D1314340

Math Lessons for Elementary Grades

Dorothy Harrer

Printed with support from the Waldorf Curriculum Fund

Published by:
Waldorf Publications at the
Research Institute for Waldorf Education
38 Main Street
Chatham, NY 12037

Title: *Math Lessons for Elementary Grades*

Author: Dorothy Harrer

Design, Layout and Cover: Hallie Jean Wootan

Editor: Hallie Jean Wootan

Illustrations: Anna Kraus
(pages 16, 25, 27, and 29)

Proofreader and Copy Editor: Charles H. Blatchford

First printed by Mercury Press in 1985
Second Printing 1990
Third Printing 1996
Fourth Printing 1998
Revised and re-edited edition by AWSNA 2005
Fifth Printing 2012
Sixth Printing by Waldorf Publications 2015

© 2005
ISBN #978-1-888365-49-8

Contents

A Selection of Lessons for the Sixth Grade

Excerpts from Rudolf Steiner

From **Practical Course for Teachers** *by Rudolf Steiner*

The reading and writing which you teach the child are determined by convention; they have arisen within the action of the physical body.

Teaching the child arithmetic is quite another thing. You will feel that here the most important thing is not the forms of the figures, but the reality that lives in the figure-forms. And this living reality is of more importance to the spiritual world than the reality living in reading and writing. And if we proceed further to teach the child certain activities which we must call artistic, we enter with them into the sphere which always has eternal significance, which reaches up into the activity of the spirit and soul in man. Our teaching is already less physical in arithmetic, and we are really teaching the soul and spirit when we teach the child music, drawing, or anything of the kind.

From **Course on Pedagogy,** *Chapter 8, by Rudolf Steiner*

If you discover a special weakness with regard to arithmetic, it will be good to do as follows: You can put those children together who are not good at arithmetic and let them have an extra hour or half-hour of gymnastics. . . . You must try to increase the powers of these children by means of gymnastics and eurythmy. First you let them do staff exercises, the staff in the hand: in front 1, 2, 3; behind 1, 2, 3, 4. Each time the child must change the position of the staff. He must make an effort in some way to get the staff behind him at 3. Then there must be running, 3 steps forward, 5 steps backward; 3 steps forward, 4 steps backward; 5 steps forward, 3 steps backward, etc. Try . . . to combine number with the child's movement, so that he is obliged to count while he is moving. Why has it an effect? . . . What lies at the root of arithmetic is consciously willed movement, the sense of movement (and it) will have the effect of bringing the child's arithmetical powers to life.

Some excerpts from **Education and Modern Spiritual Life** *by Rudolf Steiner (Lectures given at Ilkley, Yorkshire, 1923), Chapter IX, pages 158-161*

. . . everything conveyed in an external way to the child by arithmetic, or even by counting, destroys something in the human organism. To start from the unit and add to it piece by piece is simply to destroy the organism of man. But if we first awaken an awareness of the whole, then an awareness of the members of this whole—starting with the whole and then proceeding to its parts—the organism is made more alive.

First we have 1—we call this the unity. Then 2, 3, 4 and so forth are added, unit by unit, and we have no idea whatever why the one follows the other, nor of what happens in the end. . . . It is the unit which the child, too, should first see as a whole. Everything is a unity whatever it may be. Here we are obliged to illustrate it with a drawing. We must therefore draw a line; but we could use an apple just as well to do what I shall now do with a line.

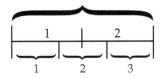

This, then, is 1. And now we go on from the whole to its parts, or members. Here, then, we have made of the 1, a 2, but the 1 still remains. And now we go on. By a further partition the 3 comes into being. Unity always remains as the all-embracing whole. . . .

We count up to 10 because we feel our members, the members of our hands. We feel our two hands symmetrically with their 10 fingers. This feeling also arises and is inwardly experienced by the child, and we must call forth the sense of number by a transition from the whole to the parts. . . . mere adding of one or more units must only be introduced as a second stage. . . .

Your teaching work will also be essentially enhanced and vivified if you similarly reverse the other simple forms of calculation. . . . Try, for instance, to bring the child to say: "If I have 7, how much must I take away to get 3," instead of "What remains over if I take 4 from 7?" That we have 7 is the real thing, and what I have left is equally real; how much must we take away from 7 to get 3? Beginning with this form of thought we stand in the midst of life, whereas with the opposite form we are face to face with an abstraction. . . . we can easily revert to the other in due course. Thus, once more, in multiplication and division we should not ask what will result when we divide 10 into two parts, but how must we divide 10 to get the number 5. . . . Here are two children—10 apples are to be divided among them. Each of them is to get 5. These are the realities. . . . Done in this way, things are always immediately adapted to life and . . . the result will be that what is frequently the usual purely external way of adding, by counting up one thing after another with a deadening effect upon arithmetic lessons, will become a vivifying force. . . .

"The Four Processes and the Temperaments," from Course on Pedagogy, given by Rudolf Steiner in 1919

How to make use of the four rules of Arithmetic in helping the Four Temperaments?

Adding is related to the phlegmatic temperament, *subtracting* to the melancholic, *multiplying* to the sanguine, *dividing*, when you work back to the dividend, to the choleric.

———————

Division is connected with subtraction, and multiplication is really only repeated addition. So you can also change about and give subtraction to the choleric child,

———————

It is very important not to go on working in a monotonous way, doing nothing but add for 6 months, etc., but where possible to take all four rules very quickly one after another and then to practice them all. You will find that this will save you a great deal of time.

———————

Addition is the arithmetical rule that is particularly suitable for phlegmatic children. Suppose I have some beans or a heap of elderberries. A child counts them and finds that there are 27 (the sum). We proceed from the sum, not from the addenda. We must now divide the whole into the addenda—into little heaps. We will have one heap of, let us say 12, another heap of 7, yet another of 3 and another of 5. Then we shall have exhausted all our elderberries, We are working out our arithmetic process with the sum 27. I should let this process be done by a number of children with a pronounced phlegmatic temperament.

$$27 = 12 + 7 + 3 + 5$$

Then because the process can be reversed, I should call up some choleric children to put the heaps together again to show that $12 + 7 + 3 + 5 = 27$.

Subtraction is pre-eminently for melancholic children when it is carried out in the following way. To the melancholic children I show a little heap of elderberries and ask them to count them. They discover there are 8 in the heap. I say, "I only want 3. How many of the elderberries must be put aside so that I shall only have 3?" They will discover that 5 must be taken away.

$$8 - ? = 3$$

I let a sanguine child do the reverse process. I ask him what has been taken away and I let him say: "If I take 5 away from 8, I shall have 3 left."

$$8 - 5 = ?$$

Multiplication. Now I take a child from the sanguine group and let him count out 56 elderberries. From them I take 8 and ask him to find out how often he will find 8 elderberries in 56. He finds that the answer is 7.

$$56 \div 8 = ?$$

Now I let the sum be done in the reverse way by the melancholic children and say: "This time I do not want to discover how often the 8 is contained in the 56, but how often you can get 7 out of it."

$$56 = ? \times 7$$

I always have the reverse process carried out by the opposite temperament.

Next I put *division* before the choleric by saying: "Look here, you have a little pile of 8; I want to know in which number you can find 8 seven times."

$$? = 7 \times 8$$

That is the form in which I use division for the choleric child (when you work back to the dividend). Then I let the phlegmatic children work out the opposite process, ordinary division.

$$56 \div ? = 8$$

So, we shall take all four rules at once and be careful that through practice they are mastered almost at the same time.

Some Thoughts in Relation to Arithmetic Teaching

When we make a pedagogical picture of the child, we can do it by showing *imagination* in the head region, *understanding* close to the heart, and *will* in the region of movement, in the limbs.

Seeing works in the upper regions most strongly, while hearing shoots down toward the will. In connection with seeing, forms such as big and little, wide and narrow, etc., affect the thinking powers while colors stir the feelings. Rhythms stir the will. Seeing and hearing can meet in the realm of feeling which forms the bridge between thought and will.

At the age of six or seven, a child is imaginative and active. We have to reach his understanding through imaginations, pictorial lessons, from one side, and from the other side through that activity which he most enjoys, the rhythmic activity. The imaginations awaken his thinking powers, the rhythmic activity strengthens his memory.

The three-fold form of a main lesson can approach the child in all the three realms of his imagination, understanding and will. The order of events can start with the rhythmic work and end with the visual, In between is the dramatic where the children become completely absorbed in the feeling content of acting something out.

Just as the daily lesson takes shape according to the being of the child, so the curriculum of the first three years develops as a child develops toward the dawning of the power of thought. The first three years are in many ways a unit. The teacher gradually emphasizes the mental work more and more as the children show signs of being able to enjoy the active element in the numbers themselves. But the active and rhythmic work is not left out.

Numbers and the Four Processes for the First Grade

Numbers

When at first we look for one,
We find it in the shining sun,

For me and you
We count one, two,
The day, the night,
The dark, the light,
The good, the bad,
The gay, the sad,
The girl, the boy
We count with joy,
They all are twos
That we can use.

Father, mother and child we see
And count them quickly: one, two, three,

That we have four seasons we know very well,
As well as four elements with which we dwell:
Fire and Water, Earth and Air
Are the four elements we share.
And four kingdoms of nature to you we can tell.

The number of fingers I have on one hand
Are one, two, three, four, five.
Five toes on each foot help me balance and stand.

Whoever counts all of his fingers knows
That he also has the same number of toes:
One, two, three, four, five, six, seven, eight, nine and ten.

We count the hours of each day
And when we do we always say:
One, two, three – four, five, six –
Seven, eight, nine – ten, eleven, twelve.

We count the months in every year
And when we do, then you will hear:
One, two, three – four, five, six –
Seven, eight, nine – ten, eleven, twelve.

The different numbers of the earth
Have been around us since our birth;
But no matter how hard we try
We cannot count all of the stars in the sky.

The Number Three

I and you
And he (or she)
Are we
In number three.

And we can see
Sun, Moon and Earth,
Another three
That ever be,

Father, Mother and Child
Are three.

Earth and Water and Air
Are everywhere for us to share.

Head, Heart and Hand
We can command
To do our will,
Good to fulfill,

The Number Three
Can take a shape
Which we can make.

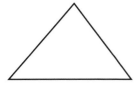

Two, Four and Eight

Eyes, ears, hands and feet –
Four pairs has everyone we meet.

Through my eyes I can see all the beauty.
Through my ears I can hear what is true.
Hands and feet will then help me show goodness
In all of the deeds that I do.

Two eyes, two ears, two hands, two feet
Are four times two in number eight.

One through Five

We live in one whole world
There numbers are unfurled.

One and two
Are I and you.
Three colors there are

That of themselves shine –
Red, Blue and Yellow.
Three others appear –
Violet, Orange and Green –
When Red blends with Blue,
Or Yellow with Red,
Or the Blue with the Yellow.

Earth gives firm rest for our feet.
Our breath comes from the air.
Water gives drink and fire heat,
Four elements give us care.

Five fingers we can count, to boot,
With five toes on each foot.

Six

6 windows there be
For you and me:

Through 2 we hear,
Through 2 we see,
1 lets us smell,
1 other tell.

2 ears that hear,
2 eyes that see,
1 nose for smelling,
1 mouth for telling
this story!

Sums

> One is one
> And stands alone.
>
> Two is one and one.
> Three is two and one.
> Four is two and two,
> But also three and one.
> In five are three and two
> And also four and one.
>
> So now our count is done.

We Are All One Whole Class

Acted out in circle

Single file

> We are all one whole class.
> One by one see us pass
> While our feet sing the song,
> Two short steps and one long.

Choose the person ahead for a partner

> Now we walk two by two
> In a ring round and true
> While our feet sing the song,
> Two short steps and one long.

The teacher chooses three children far apart in the circle, giving them the number names One, Two *and* Three

> In we run, merrily,
> One to Two, Two to Three,
> Three to where One should be

All in circle again

> While our feet sing the song
> Two short steps and one long.

The teacher chooses four children in the same way to run a square

> Run a square and count four—
> One ———, two ———, three ———
> And one more ———.

All

> While our feet sing the song,
> Two short steps and one long.

All standing in circle with arms and legs out-stretched

> We are stars full of light
> With five rays shining bright
> In the dark sky at night,

Moving hand in hand

> While our feet sing the song,
> Two short steps and one long.

Gnomes and Jewels

Deep, underground, the gnomes are always busy working to gather jewels for the Gnome King's Treasure House. Every gnome has to bring in exactly 12 jewels every day, no more, no less, for most of them can only count to 12; but there are four gnomes who can count more, and fewer, and this makes them act differently. They even look different from their ordinary companions! Two of these fellows usually come home with more than 12 jewels and the other two with fewer.

Times is the name of the first. Yellow as a candle flame, he lights up hidden places so as to find more treasure, at least 2 times more than 12 jewels a day. And he has to make two trips, instead of one, to be able to show off before all the others bragging, "Twice as much I bring to please my King!"

Plus is the second gnome, fat, green and greedy. He loves to think, "3 and 3 and 3 and 3 are twelve" and as he adds up what he finds, he wants more and more not only for the King but for himself. He fills his hands and stuffs his pants so that they rattle as he approaches the King. When he gives the King only 12 of his pretty stones, the King hears his rattling pants and turns *Plus* upside-down to get all the rest. Says *Plus*, "My pants I pad with all I add."

Minus, the third gnome, is blue and ragged. He has holes in his suit and holes in the sack which he carries. The jewels he gathers fall out through the holes as he wails, "Raggedy-blue, what will I do?" He always has fewer than he should even when he meets one who is always willing to share what he has found and consequently also has fewer.

Warm-hearted and red as the heart's blood, the fourth gnome is named *Division*. When he hears the wailing of blue *Minus*, he hurries up to him saying, "With you I'll share the jewels I bear."

Now the Gnome King knows all about these four gnomes. He knows that Minus will always be losing his jewels but that *Plus* will find them and add them to his pile. The King knows that *Division* will have fewer because he is kind enough to divide up his jewels and give a share to *Minus*; and that although *Division* brings in only a part of what he is supposed to, *Times* will bring in more than he should so that in the end nothing is lost but some is gained.

If—
Minus loses 8 and has 4 left
and—
Plus picks up the 8 and adds them to his 12
and—
Division gives 6 to *Minus* and keeps 6
and—
Times gathers 2 times 12 how many jewels do they bring in altogether?

The Four Processes

One can, in reciting and acting out these verses, draw upon the temperaments of the children: *Division* as choleric, *Plus* as phlegmatic, *Minus* the melancholic and *Multiplication* as the sanguine (adapted by D.H. from similar verses by Margaret Peckham).

Division is a kind old gnome.
With each one he will share.
The jewels which he gathers
He divides with greatest care.

 ÷

Plus keeps whatever he can find.
Each hand holds quite a heap.
He adds the jewels together
And says, "They're mine to keep."

 +

Minus is such a careless gnome.
He loses everything.
His ragged bag is empty
For he subtracts everything.

 —

Multiplication knows quite well
That 2 times 2 makes 4.
He always likes to multiply
So that he'll have much more.

 ×

The Family that Became One Person:
A Story for the Number 8

Once upon a time there was a beautiful palace built in an earthly meadow by unseen hands. The palace tower was covered with a perfect dome as round as the earth itself and through the windows in the tower one could see and hear far and wide in all directions. Within the palace were many rooms and passageways for work and play.

One day a family of children was brought to live in the palace by a giant nurse who was so much larger than the palace that she could not get into it with the children but had to care for them from the outside. She made short journeys to market to get them food and drink; but the rest of the time she stayed on guard outside to keep trouble away from the door.

People wondered if the children had a father or a mother. No one could find out where they had come from or who had built their palace. Moreover it was such a large family that people wondered at it even more. There were eight children altogether and every two were twins. Four pairs of twins! Each pair not only looked alike but each pair liked to do the same kind of thing.

The youngest twins were boys. They liked to run and play all the time. They didn't want to be still at all, as long as they were awake, and the giantess often saw them kick each other and step on each other's toes in their rough games.

The next youngest twins were gentler. They were girls. They always played together happily, building sand castles, gathering flowers and dressing their dolls. Their hands were always busy.

The next pair were always sitting by two of the tower windows. They were also girls. Being older, they did not feel like playing. They liked to keep their windows open and listen to the wind play soft music in the trees. When they heard the songs of birds or the voices of people talking and laughing in the distance, they wondered when someone would come to bring an important message just for them.

The oldest of the twins were boys. They, too, stayed up in the tower peering out of two other windows to look at what was going on in the outside world. They liked to watch the sunrise and the sunset, to see the colors of the flowers in the fields, to look far away to the roofs and steeples of the distant towns. They would have liked to take hold of all they saw, to claim it all as their very own, but they could not bring themselves down from the tower.

So it was that these four pairs of twins, living together inside their palace in such separate ways, had all to be taken care of by the giant-ess because they did not take care of each other. The twins in the tower never came downstairs and the two younger girls and the two younger boys hardly knew that there was anybody upstairs.

Time passed and the people around who knew about the strange family, in the beautiful palace, wondered more and more about what would finally happen, because sensible human beings know that children have to learn how to take care of themselves and help each other.

All this while a great and good King was journeying in search of his children. It seemed to be an endless journey, quite as far as from heaven to earth. The children had been carried away from their home-land by giants who wanted to win power over the King.

The King took no armies or weapons with him but he had a posses-sion that was of more value than ten thousand armed men. This was a magical cloak that covered him from head to toe. Wearing this he was able to travel unharmed through each of the four elements; through rocks, through water, through wind and fire; and he was able to do so without being seen.

Not even the old giantess, on guard by the twins' palace, could see him as he passed her and went in through the gate. He made his way through all the passageways and rooms up to the very dome and was overjoyed to find all of his twin children there.

How were the King and his twins to escape from the giant nurse who guarded their palace-prison? All eight of the children couldn't get under his magic cloak. The King brought them all together in the heart of the palace and taught them how they could help each other.

Thus spoke the King to the four older children: "Since you know how to look and listen, you must become the eyes and ears for your younger brothers and sisters."

Then to the four younger ones he said, "Since you have such busy hands and feet, you must become the limbs for your older brothers and sisters and help them move out into the world."

Then to all of them he said, "If you do this you will become like one person and can enter into my magic cloak with me."

Thus the four pairs of twins became like one person. The King cast his cloak around them and guided then past the giant nurse to begin their return journey to their homeland.

A Selection of Lessons for the Second Grade

The Richest Number

Once upon a time various numbers were moving about in a beautiful number palace where many steps led up to a golden throne. Each of the numbers wanted to sit on the throne, rule over the other numbers, and be the most important one. Not one of them wanted to say, "I am not as great as you are."

Number One said, "I stand first before all of you!
To me the royal throne is due.
When we are counted, you will see
That all of you just follow me."

"I don't agree," said Number Two,
"for I am more than you!"

Number Four
stamped on the floor
and gave a roar,
"I am more
than One or Two!"

And Six cried out,
"What's this about?
Just look at me
and you will see!"

Eight shouted, "I'm as rich as Six
and do as many tricks."

Number Nine said, "That is fine
but I am higher in the line!"

Then Number Twelve said, "Let us see
how many numbers there will be
in all of me."

Thirteen claimed he should be King
For he had more of everything.

Suggestion: The children can be asked, "Which of these numbers should be King?" They can be told to think it over for the next day. They accept such an assignment enthusiastically. The next lesson can start with the question, "Would the King be richer or poorer than his subjects?" Then the following study can be worked through at the blackboard to be copied into their notebooks by the class.

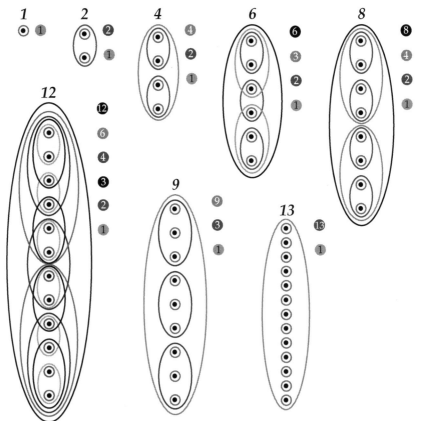

Beginning with the ones, the numbers are gradually encircled and appear as crown jewels, to the side. 12 appears as the richest of these numbers.

The Richest Number (continued in another lesson)

Now that 12 was King, he ordered all lesser numbers to share, equally, with him the work of his kingdom.

First, he proclaimed that they had 6 days for work and the 7th for rest. At least 2 of the numbers had to be in command on each of the 6 days.

$$2 + 2 + 2 + 2 + 2 + 2 = 12$$

Next, they had to divide up equally into 2 groups of guards to guard the King's palace by day and by night.

$$6 + 6 = 12$$

Then they had to divide into 3 equal groups for 3 kinds of jobs:

- Reading from Books of Wisdom
- Singing Songs of Joy
- Marching in Palace Parades

$$4 + 4 + 4 = 12$$

They had to divide into 4 groups for 4 different occupations:

$$3 + 3 + 3 + 3 = 12$$

- Ploughing the earth
- Making fire in the stoves
- Carrying water from the wells
- Airing the rooms of the palace

Finally, they had to divide up so that there was someone to stand in the palace tower and call out each hour of the day.

$$1 + 1 + 1 + 1 + 1 + 1 + 1 + 1 + 1 + 1 + 1 + 1 = 12$$

And that was the way King Twelve shared the work of his kingdom!

(These number combinations can also be practiced in division and multiplication, i.e., $12 = 6 \times 2$ and $\frac{6}{2\overline{)12}}$ etc.

Odd and Even Numbers

Note: When the form of a lesson is such that it starts with activity, goes over to object counting and then writing, the children are helped to concentrate and to bring into their thinking what they have learned through their limbs, breath, and dramatic feeling.

Active Arithmetic

The children stand facing each other in two rows. Opposites hold hands as partners and are given number names. Each pair repeats its numbers:

> 1 has 2 for a partner
>
> 3 has 4 for a partner
>
> 5 has 6 for a partner
>
> 7 has 8 for a partner
>
> 9 has 10 for a partner, etc.

They see, and learn, that when the two sides are "even" they all have partners. If there is one without a partner, that one is "odd." If the teacher calls "7," all numbers above 7 sit down; i.e. 8, 9, 10 sit down. Then 7 is seen to be odd and the children chant, "7 is an odd number." If the teacher calls "4," all numbers above 4 sit down. 1 and 3 still stand facing 2 and 4. All have partners and the children chant, "4 is an even number." This can be very quick and active and the children learn to think fast when they have to decide whether they stand or sit. In the end the children can be asked to say their own numbers by sides—1, 3, 5, 7, 9 and 2, 4, 6, 8, 10—and thus find that on one side are the "odd" numbers while on the other are the "even" numbers, Then the odd numbers can form a little circle to move around counting and stepping between the odd numbers: 1-step-3-step-5-step, etc. Then the even numbers can do likewise. Gradually they practice counting without stepping between the numbers.

Object Counting (with beans, shells, acorns, etc.)

Odd and *even* teams sit facing each other across desks. The teacher gives the *odds* an odd number of beans and gives the *evens* an even number. Each *odd* then gives the opposite *even* enough beans to make the *even* odd and the *odd* even. Or *evens* can give *odds* enough to make them even, and to become odd themselves. The teacher can work out variations.

Written Work

In the following number pattern the children write the lowest row first, making the odd numbers blue and the even numbers red. Then, directly over each odd number they write 1 in blue, the color for the odd numbers. Next, they write 2 in red over every even number (red for *even*).

$$0 \ 0 \ 2 \ 2 \ 4 \ 4 \ 6 \ 6 \ 8 \ 8$$

$$1 \ 2 \ 1 \ 2 \ 1 \ 2 \ 1 \ 2 \ 1 \ 2$$

$$1 \ 2 \ 3 \ 4 \ 5 \ 6 \ 7 \ 8 \ 9 \ 10$$

The top row appears as they write the answers, reading upward from the bottom row, to the questions:

> 1 is 1 plus what?
>
> 2 is 2 plus what?
>
> 3 is 1 plus what?
>
> 4 is 2 plus what?
>
> and so forth.

They enjoy finding that the whole top row, except for the zeros, appears in red and in a definite sequence of the 2-table.

Dictation

Numbers can be dictated at random with the children writing them in blue or red according to whether they are odd or even. Later simple examples can be dictated and the children told to use blue and red to show the odd and even.

Big Smoke and Little Flame

Note: As the teacher tells this story, it can be illustrated and the number stories written on the blackboard for the class to copy. The children should take part in working out the number stories.

Big Smoke was a gray squirrel who could skin up the tallest trees and leap from branch to branch, flying almost like a bird and never missing his foothold on the next branch.

Little Flame was a red chipmunk who darted about over the ground like fire and burrowed deep underground to make her winter home below the snow and ice.

It was October and both were working busily to find and store away nuts and acorns and seeds in secret places for their winter feasts. Big Smoke stored nuts in hollow trees and also among the roots of grasses. Little Flame stored what she gathered underground in tunnel rooms that she made.

One morning, not long ago, they both gathered some hazelnuts in about one hour. Altogether they had found 12 nuts. Big Smoke had been luckier than Little Flame. He had found and stored away 5 nuts. Little Flame had found and stored 4 nuts.

Then, as Big Smoke went forth to look for more, Little Flame found 2 of the nuts that Big Smoke had hidden. She put them in her store room together with her 4. Now she had __?__.

Of the 8 that Big Smoke had hidden, he now had only __?__ left.

Now they each had an equal amount of the 12!

And now that she had found Big Smoke's stores, Little Flame let him do the hunting while she raided his hiding places. She could stuff a lot in her cheeks and pocketed 4 more of his nuts. Now she had __?__ nuts and he was left with __?__. How many times more did she have than he?

When she went back to get his last 2 nuts, he chased her away with a good scolding; but he could not get back that which she had taken because he could not get into her tunnels. He was too big.

Practice Work in Object Counting, Drawing and Writing
Suggestion: Each child can take part in this at the same time once the nuts are given out. The left hand can be Big Smoke *and the right hand can be*

Little Flame, *each one handling and arranging the nuts in relation to the story and variations.*

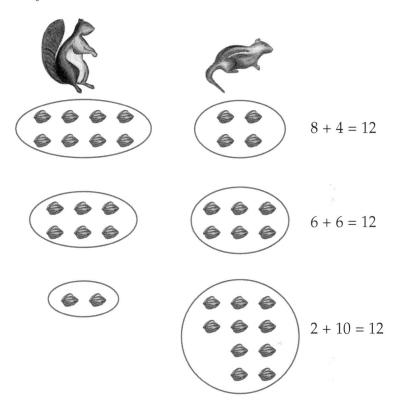

$$8 + 4 = 12$$

$$6 + 6 = 12$$

$$2 + 10 = 12$$

Multiplication Play for Second Graders

Note: Written for 20 children, but adaptable for any number. Characters: Gates (10), Treasure Hunters and Finders (10).

The Gates stand in a circle and the Treasure Hunters stand outside. The Gates face outward and wear soft silk scarves attached to their wrists, in various colors, with paper caps to match; Treasure Hunters wear caps of a single color.

Gates: Ten gates a treasure guard!
To open them is not so hard

> For each gate provides a key
> That will unlock the mystery.

Treasure Hunters: We seek this hidden treasure
> And it will give us pleasure.
> Our only claim,
> So far, to fame
> Is that we each
> Have the same name,
> and that is "2".
> (or 3, or 4, or 5, etc.)

One by one, the Treasure Hunters approach a Gate.

Treasure Hunter: Here I stand,
> May I go through?

Gate: I am 2 (or 4, or 6, or 8, etc.)
> Who are you?

Treasure Hunter: I am 2! (etc.)

Gate: Then bow one time
> And you may go through.

2 goes through 2, after one bow, and stands inside the circle

Treasure Hunter: 2 is 1 times 2.
> (etc., and then is followed by the
> other Treasure Hunters, up to 10 times,
> until all are in the circle.)

Treasure Hunter: Now, all hidden treasure
> We can truly measure,
> The keys that led us to our stations
> Were just 10 easy multiplications.

All:

$2 = 1 \times 2$

$4 = 2 \times 2$

$6 = 3 \times 2$ etc., up to 10×2, or whatever table has been acted out.

Closed Gates   Open Gates

Two Shapes: An Introduction to the Four-Table

There are two shapes in this world who are not at all like each other. One day they made friends and told each other what was bothering them.

The first one said, "When I stand up, I can never stay still. I have to keep moving and get so tired that I fall flat!"

The other said, "That's nothing. When I stand up, I can't go anywhere. I try hard but I just get stuck and fall flat too!"

"Well," said the first one, "it would be fun to be able to just stand still even for a moment. It would be a change for me."

The second one answered, "I'd give anything to be able to just stand up and roll along."

What do you think these shapes were like?

Note: At this point the teacher can ask the children to take out paper and pencils and draw each shape as they think it might be.

Many of you have had the right idea! (A few had drawn triangles rather than squares. The teacher now shows a red cardboard circle who rolls along and a green cardboard square who can't roll and run but stands for a moment on its base, gets tired and falls flat.)

Well, the circle invited the square to get inside the circle and go for a ride. (This time a square has had to be cut to fit within the circle and can be made to stick to it with Scotch Tape or rubber cement.)

"Oh," cried the circle after rolling a short distance and falling flat, "I do get tired rolling around and wish I could stand still and be quiet for a moment."

"That's easy. I'll help you," said the square. "I'll make myself bigger and let you get inside of me."

So the square enlarged itself so that the circle could just fit into it (a second larger square is used). Then the square stood up straight and strong without rolling.

"What a pleasure!" cried the circle. "You keep me from rolling around."

"Alas," sobbed the square, "my strength and balance have given out."

Then they both fell flat.

Drawing

Have the children draw the circle within the square, free-hand.

Written Work

The square is the shape of the four-table. It has four equal sides.

$$4 = 1 \times 4$$
$$8 = 2 \times 4$$
$$12 = 3 \times 4$$

(etc. to 48)

The King's Advisors

(Adapted from a story by Margaret Peckham)

Once upon a time there was a young King who ruled over a large kingdom. He was very rich. His large treasure chamber was chock full of bags of gold and precious stones. He was known to be the richest King in all the world yet he was not happy. His subjects did not like him because he looked so cross and miserable and they called him names like King Crosspatch or His Miserable Majesty.

No King, however rich, can rule his kingdom well if he doesn't feel happy. And this young King knew that but he didn't know what to do about it. If only there were someone to advise him and tell him what to do so that he would be happy and his subjects would like him!

At last he decided to call for an advisor. He ordered his heralds to blow their trumpets from the four towers of his palace. This was the signal for all the people to gather together.

Then the heralds called out in all four directions, "Hear ye! Hear ye! Hear ye! Hear ye! His Majesty is seeking an advisor who will help him rule wisely and well. He who shows himself to be a good advisor will never want for anything the rest of his life!"

It was not long before there was a knocking at the palace gate. Hearing it, the King told his servants to open the gate. He took his place on the throne as a strange man entered the throne room to stand before the King. Such a strange man, all clothed in dark blue! He was long and thin with a long thin nose, long thin fingers, a thin line of a mouth and long thin hair; and even a long, thin sign on his sleeve.

He bowed respectfully before the King and said, "Sire, I have come to advise you as to how to rule your kingdom wisely and well."

"What is your name?" asked the King.

"My name," said the man, pointing to the sign on his sleeve, "is Subtraction."

Then the King told Subtraction that, in spite of all his riches, he was most unhappy.

Subtraction answered, "All your gold and precious stones will never make you happy. Let me take them away. Then you will be as happy as a bird who flies and sings with joy all day long."

The King was glad to be so advised and he let Subtraction take away all the bags of gold and jewels until not one was left. Then, before he departed, Subtraction put his sign "–" on the King's throne.

Now the King tried to feel happy so that his people would love him. Instead he began to feel hungry because he had no more money to buy food for his table. Day after day he got hungrier and thinner and crosser. Finally he decided that Subtraction had given him very poor advice, so he told his heralds to sound their trumpets and call for a new advisor.

The next strange man who came looked very kind and generous. He wore a warm red cloak and on his sleeve appeared a sign, "÷." As he bowed before the King, the King asked him why he looked so warm and kind.

The man answered, "Because I share all that I have with others."

"What is your name?"asked the King.

"I am called Division because when I share, I divide." Then the King told him how Subtraction had taken away all the royal treasure so that he had nothing left to buy food for his table.

"Oh that Subtraction!" said Division. "He is my brother and I know him well. He never has anything left to share because he loses all that he gets. I will find what he has taken away from you and help you to divide it up and share it with all of your subjects. Then you will be happy, and they will love you."

As he left, Division put his sign on the King's throne, "÷." He soon came back again, bringing the King all the treasure Subtraction had taken away. He helped the King divide it up and share it with all the people in the kingdom

This left the King with only his share, which was very small, not enough to buy grain for his horses and meat for his hunting dogs. So he decided that Division's advice was not good enough.

Once more the King commanded his heralds to sound their trumpets and call for a new advisor.

Now came a very slow-acting, fat man as green and as round as a cabbage. He seemed to roll in but like a ball that wanted to stop rolling. On his fat arm with its tight sleeve appeared the sign "+."

"What is your name?"asked the King as the fat man stood before him, unable to bow because he was too fat and round.

"My name," said the man, puffing out his cheeks, "is Addition because I like to keep adding to what I have."

The King told Addition how Division had arranged for him to share so much of his wealth with the people of his kingdom that there was not enough left to buy grain for his horses and meat for his hunting dogs.

"I will help you!" said Addition who then called all of the King's people together. They came willingly, hoping that the King had something more to share with them. Addition told the people that, having shared so much of his wealth with them, his own share was too small to buy food for his horses and hunting dogs.

Then the people, who loved to see their King and all his courtiers riding by on their prancing steeds with their dogs to hunt for game, brought back all the gold and jewels to the King's treasure chamber where Addition piled it all up again until the King had as much as he had begun with. Then Addition put his sign "+" on the King's throne and advised the King to keep all his riches.

Once again, the King was rich, the people felt poor, and everyone was unhappy.

"Oh dear," cried the King, "I am right back where I started from. What shall I do?"

For the fourth time he commanded his heralds to sound out their trumpets and call for another advisor; and in answer there appeared a fourth person who shone like a yellow flame. He danced here and there, never staying in one place, and on his sleeve there zig-zagged a sign "×." He criss-crossed about all the while he listened to the King and answered him.

When the King told the dancing one how things had turned out, the flame-like one answered, "You will never have enough for yourself and your people and for your horses and dogs unless you follow my advice."

"What is your name?" asked the King.

I am Multiplication, and my advice is that you turn everything that you have into more by multiplying it."

Multiplication now drew his sign on the King's throne and then invited the King to come along with him for a walk. Multiplication led the King into the countryside beyond the city and showed him an apple tree. He advised the King to plant many more apple trees so as to multiply the apple crop. He showed him a cornfield and advised him to make many more cornfields to multiply the corn crop. He showed him a vegetable garden and advised him to plant many more such gardens so as to multiply crops of vegetables.

When the King carried out the advice of Multiplication, he harvested more than he knew what to do with. He had to build all kinds of storage bins and towers to keep the extra produce and even then a lot of it spoiled and rotted away.

Now the King, in despair, left his palace and his kingdom to journey afar and to try to forget his troubles and his advisors.His wanderings led him into a pathless wilderness where he would have become forever lost and forgotten, except there appeared to him, one day, an old woman who gazed at him as if she know all that was happening.

She said to him, "Well, Your Majesty, I see you have found your advisors!"

With that, she disappeared and the King turned around and went back to his kingdom, for he had begun to understand what she meant.

Then he reached home, he called for Subtraction, Division, Addition and Multiplication and asked all four to become his advisors.

Upon the advice of Lord Multiplication all the people worked to multiply everything they needed and brought what was left over to the King. Count Addition added it all together so that the Duke of Division could divide the surplus wealth equally for Sir Subtraction to take away and give each of the people his share while leaving a remainder for the King.

So it was that the four Advisors helped the King become rich and share his wealth so that he and his people were happy forever after.

Practicing the Eight Table

Eight soldiers guard a dungeon. Within their circle is a prisoner. He has to know the right password to get out of the dungeon. The soldiers are numbers 8, 16, 24, 32, 40, 48, 56 and 64. The prisoner is number 8.

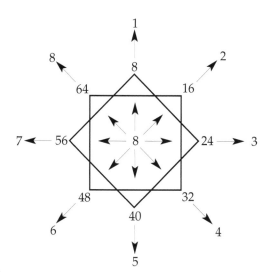

Eight has to go to number 8, first, and number 8 says,

"Give me the password true
And I will let you through."

Eight stamps once and is allowed to go out to be number 1 in a new circle. Soldier 8 now has to go into the dungeon and try to get out by going to soldier 16 who says,

"Give me the password true
And I will let you through."

The new *Eight* stamps twice and is allowed to go out to be number 2 in the new circle, while 16 goes into the dungeon and becomes *Eight*.

This third *Eight* has to stamp 3 times to get out through number 24 and become 3 in the new circle, and so on until number 64 has been captured inside the dungeon. (The above drawing can be given as notebook work.)

The Nine Table

(An Assembly Demonstration)

Ten children wearing numerals 0 through 9 stand in a row. Others of the class can stand to one side to join in the recitation. The "numbers" move forward from the row to stand side by side, then again come forward to exchange places as new numbers when the digits are reversed.

"We have learned the 9 table,
　　And the secret of number nine
You will find when you are able
　　To see how we combine."

0　1　2　3　4　5　6　7　8　9

0	9	"is 1 times nine"
1	8	"is 2 times nine"
2	7	"is 3 times nine"
3	6	"is 4 times nine"
4	5	"is 5 times nine"

"This is not the only secret we have found
For each pair of numbers to the 9 is bound."

(After each of the next lines is spoken, the numbers move to the rear and change places to complete the progression.)

$$9 + 0 = 9$$
$$8 + 1 = 9$$
$$7 + 2 = 9$$
$$6 + 3 = 9$$
$$5 + 4 = 9$$
$$4 + 5 = 9$$
$$3 + 6 = 9$$
$$2 + 7 = 9$$
$$1 + 8 = 9$$
$$0 + 9 = 9$$

(Now the numbers go back to their places in a row from 0 to 9 and the class counts by ones to nine and back.)

"0 1 2 3 4 5 6 7 8 9, 9 8 7 6 5 4 3 2 1   0"

The Ten Table

Hold up the first finger on the right hand as #1. The fingers on each hand follow until the left thumb pops up as 10, and so on, with the left thumb showing the change from 10 to 20 to 30, etc.

What are the names of the left thumb each time? (through 100) Write them on the blackboard, as in the first line below. Then keep going through 990:

10	20	30	40	50	60	70	80	90	100
110	120	130	140	150	160	170	180	190	200
210	220	230	240	250	260	270	280	290	300
310	320	330	340	350	360	370	380	390	400
410	420	430	440	450	460	470	480	490	500
510	520	530	540	550	560	570	580	590	600
610	620	630	640	650	660	670	680	690	700
710	720	730	740	750	760	770	780	790	800
810	820	830	840	850	860	870	880	890	900
910	920	930	940	950	960	970	980	990	?

What can you see in the number pattern? What part of the numbers in each column remains the same? (10, 20, 30, etc.) What numbers change? (1 hundred, 2 hundred, 3 hundred, etc.)

What would come next after 990? 10 hundred!

10 hundred can be written as 10,00, but is usually written as 1,000 and called 1 thousand. Who can follow the number pattern of the 10 table through the thousands?

Linear (Line) Measure

Activity: Have various children measure, with their feet end to end, the distance from one side of the blackboard to the other, marking some of the feet on the floor with chalk. Call attention to the fact that some of the feet are shorter than others. Point out that a man's foot is a more reliable measure because he is full grown and his foot won't grow any longer as would a child's.

With his feet, a man can measure lengths from one place or point to another. The length of a man's foot has been made into a measure called a "foot." You will find this "foot" on your new rulers.

To measure something smaller than a foot a shorter measure is needed, maybe a toe or a finger joint. For instance, the length of my thumb from the tip to the first knuckle just about fits into my ruler 12 times (*Demonstrate*). This magic and rich number fits into a foot just right. Every foot ruler is divided into what grown-ups call inches (jointses!). In each foot there are 12 inches.

Notebook Work

Have each child make a tracing of his ruler and color it, then write under it,

This is a foot

Under that have them rule a 1-inch line and write, beneath it,

This is 1 inch

Letter the "rule,"

There are 12 inches in a foot

1 foot = 12 inches

By way of review, in the next lesson, the children can measure with their foot rulers various objects such as books, pencil boxes, and desks, to find out how long and how wide they are in feet and/or inches. Then, also with the foot rulers, they can measure the length and width of the classroom. They find that this is a tedious task. Now the yardstick is introduced.

If we want to measure longer lengths than a foot or two, we can use a longer measure. The next longer measure to a foot could be a leg, or an arm. The distance from your nose to your fingertip is about three times as long as your foot, about 3 feet. A measure that is 3 feet long is called a yard. Show a yardstick. Compare its length with various arms and legs not yet "full grown." Compare a foot ruler with the yardstick. Now they can measure the room with the yardstick to find that the task is done more quickly, They should be helped to convert the room's length and/or width from yards, feet and inches into feet and inches.

Notebook Work (to write)

>1 yard = 3 feet
>3 feet = 3 × 12 inches = 36 inches
>1 yard = 36 inches

Simple Examples

2 × 3 = 6	2 yards = 6 feet
3 × 3 = 9	3 yards = 9 feet
4 × 3 = 12	4 yards = 12 feet

Time Rhymes

Sixty seconds make a minute.
Put a lot of kindness in it.
Sixty minutes make an hour.
Work with all your might and power.
Twelve bright hours make a day,
Time enough for work and play.
Twelve dark hours through the night
Give us sleep till morning light.
Seven days a week will make.
This we'll learn if pains we take.
Four to five weeks make the months.
Remember this or be a dunce.
Twelve long months will make a year,
In one of them your birthday, dear.

(old rhyme)
"Thirty days hath September,
April, June and November.

All the rest have thirty-one
But February stands alone,
Twenty-eight is his full share
With 29 in each leap year."

In each year are seasons four.
We will see them we are sure,
Spring and Summer, then the Fall,
Winter last but best of all.

A Number Story for the Six Table

(as done in a Second Grade)

This story accompanies the drawing of the hexagon, free-hand, in steps I through VII, as illustrated.

Step I

There was once a King whose shining palace was right in the center of his six-sided kingdom. At each side of the kingdom rose a high wall and each of the six walls was one of six beautiful colors: violet, blue, green, yellow, orange, and red.

Although these six beautiful walls protected him from all enemies, they limited his kingdom to what they enclosed and beyond them the King had no power nor did he know what lay beyond them.

Step II

Strangely enough, the King had just six sons. When they had grown up to become noble knights, they rode out from the King's palace in six different directions in order to explore the kingdom.

At length each reached a corner between each of the six walls and each looked to his right to see a wall built of violet, blue, green, yellow, orange, or red. But beyond that they could not go.

Whereupon they returned to the King and asked him what lay beyond the walls of the kingdom.

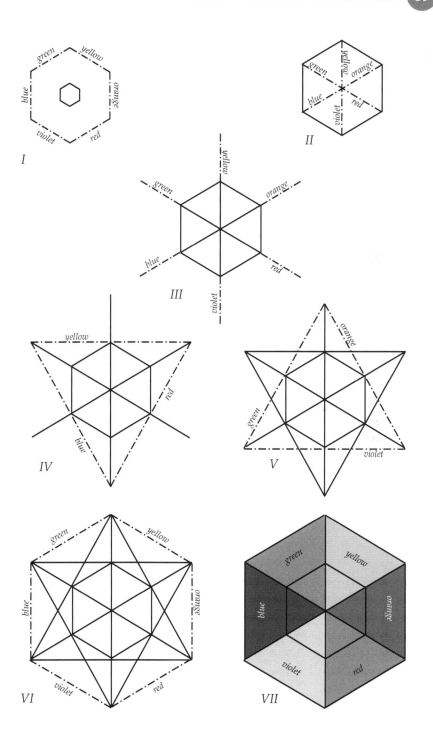

I

II

III

IV

V

VI

VII

The King answered, "I know not for although the six walls protect me from my enemies, they do not permit me to see what lies beyond them. I have had enough to do to rule my kingdom wisely, and well within its six walls, and here I must stay. Now you have my blessing to find your way beyond the walls and to carry my good will to all that live without."

Step III

Thereupon, each knight chose a banner of a color to match the wall he had seen and each set out with fluttering banner and sound of trumpet to breach the wall.

Upon reaching the corner, each young knight with the help of his trusty men broke through the walls and marched forth into the world beyond his father's kingdom.

Step IV

The yellow knight traveled as far outside the walls as it was from the palace to the walls. He found himself in a desert blazing with hot sun and sand, no living being, no plant nor animal in sight. So he returned to the wall and looked to the right and to the left. Seeing in the distance his red and blue brothers, he went straight to meet the red then back to meet the blue who likewise had journeyed beyond their corners then returned to the old walls. The blue knight had found himself facing a deep, blue ocean which he could not cross and the red knight was turned back by a sea of red fire. Yellow, Red and Blue each built a new wall, straight and sure, touching at three points on the old. Along the new walls they set up lines of their trusty henchmen to guard their father's kingdom against blinding light, bottomless ocean and searing fire.

Step V

In the meantime the orange, violet and green knights had each journeyed out from the corners where the walls of the kingdom met. They too went as far out as their brothers. The orange faced a shimmering heat, the violet a bottomless pit and the green an endless sea of green grass. They too returned to build new walls which touched upon the old.

Step VI

Now all six knights gained courage arid joined forces. The red set up a defense and built a red wall from the violet to the orange to better guard the kingdom against the burning fire. Now he, especially, felt great courage within his own being. The violet knight built a wall from red to blue. From its ramparts he prayed and found the endless reaches of eternity where he could look beyond the bottomless pit to realms where there were never any endings. Blue stretched his ramparts from violet to green and built his wall deep and strong against the deep, blue ocean. Once done, he felt calm, peaceful and sure that no storm could enter his father's kingdom. Green built his new wall from blue to yellow. Outside that wall great grasses and jungles crowded toward the inner kingdom but could not enter through the wall.

But from his wall, green could look far in understanding how all life was linked together. Yellow built a wall of golden light against the blinding desert sun. It was a wall of wisdom that guarded his father's kingdom against all that dazzles and dizzies those who have no wisdom. It made the outer light dim in the strength of an inner light. And lastly, orange built a wall that guarded the kingdom from the heat that flickered between the desert and the fire. The orange wall established, within the kingdom, a power of warm-hearted love in everyone of the subjects of the King.

Step VII

Each knight, having had his part in enlarging the old kingdom to become four times its original size, lets each color enter the spirit of the realm:

with yellow came wisdom	(knowing what to do)
with red came courage	(doing what is hard)
with blue came peace	(a feeling of God's love for mankind)
with green came understanding	(of others)
with violet came a sense of eternity	(timelessness)
with orange came love	(for all that is good).

Keeping Track of Numbers—Counting Exercises

Note: Exercises such as these can, at first, be done in unison with the teacher. When the class is familiar with the number progressions, every other one can be in response either to the teacher or to one part of the group.

2 4 6 8	→	8 6 4
4 6 8 10	→	10 8 6
6 8 10 12	→	12 10 8
8 10 12 14	→	14 12 10 etc.

2 4 6 8
  4 6 8 10
    6 8 10 12
      8 10 12 14
        10 12 14 16
          12 14 16 18
            14 16 18 20

You may think this plenty!

            16 18 20 22
              18 20 22 24

But there are ever more
Beyond the 24!!

2 4 6 8
    8 6 2 4
      4 6 8 10
        10 8 4 6
          6 8 10 12
            12 10 6 8   etc.

2 4 6 8 10
    10 6 8 2 4
      4 6 8 10 12
        12 8 10 4 6   etc.

Another Counting Exercise

1 2 3 4	→	4 3 1 2
2 3 4 5	→	5 4 2 3
3 4 5 6	→	6 5 3 4
4 5 6 7	→	7 6 4 5
5 6 7 8	→	8 7 5 6
6 7 8 9	→	9 8 6 7
7 8 9 10	→	Now we go back again.

10 9 7 8
9 8 6 7
8 7 5 6
7 6 4 5
6 5 3 4
5 4 2 3
4 3 1 2
3 2 0 1
And with one
We are done!

The Giant Who Counted with his Feet

There was once a Giant who could count with his feet much better than he could count with his voice. He was so good at counting that he never made a mistake even though he did it with his feet.

A King, who heard of the Giant and of how good he was in arithmetic, invited him to come to the palace. When the Giant came before the King, the King asked him four questions:

1. I have five sons who are about to go forth into the world to see its sights. Before they go I want to give them each a gift. Here are 25 gold pieces. How many should I give to each son so that he will have an equal share? The Giant answered with 5 steps. (Teacher does it.)

$$5\overline{)25}^{\,5}$$

2. I have five daughters. They have to stay at home but to make them happy I want to give them each 2 pearls. How many pearls should I get from my treasure house? The Giant answered with 10 steps.

$$5 \times 2 = 10$$

3. I have five counselors. I want to give them each a book of wisdom in return for their wise words but I have only 3 books to give. How many counselors would not receive a book? The giant answered with 2 steps.

$$5 - 3 = 2$$

4. Here is my chief hunter with his bow and arrows. I see that he has only 20 arrows. If I give him 5 more, how many will he have? The Giant answered with 25 steps.

$$20 + 5 = 25$$

The King wanted to test the giant with harder number questions. (Now the children take turns as the Giant, with their feet.)

$30 = ? \times 5$	$5 + 5 = ?$	$35 - 30 = ?$	$5\overline{)30}^{\,?}$
$15 = ? \times 5$	$3 + 2 = ?$	$15 - 5 = ?$	$5\overline{)15}^{\,?}$
$15 = 3 \times ?$	$2 + ? = 6$	$12 - 5 = ?$	$5\overline{)20}^{\,?}$
$20 = ? \times 5$	$5 + 10 = ?$	$8 - 5 = ?$	$2\overline{)10}^{\,?}$
$20 = 5 \times ?$	$5 + 3 = ?$	$? - 5 = 2$	$3\overline{)15}^{\,?}$
$50 = 10 \times ?$	$5 + 4 = ?$	$9 - 4 = ?$	$5\overline{)40}^{\,?}$

When the King heard the giant's feet tramping and counting without making any mistakes, he was so pleased that he invited the Giant to live in his palace and be his chief Counter!

Practice in counting with the feet. (In succeeding lessons.)
Many giants were carrying bags of rocks up a mountain, 100 steps. At the top of the mountain they emptied all their bags in one pile of 100 rocks. Then each giant threw a number of rocks down into a lake at the bottom of the mountain, counting and subtracting till all the rocks were gone. Then each giant jumped part way down the mountain, 80 or so jumps, and walked the remaining steps (20 etc.) Those who couldn't count the remaining steps correctly had to go back and be rescued. If they still couldn't or didn't count the steps of the rescuer, they couldn't get down and were counted "out."

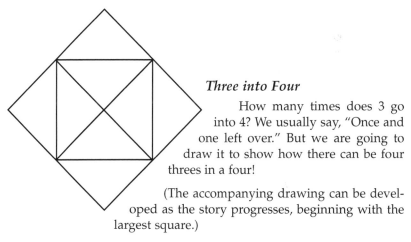

Three into Four

How many times does 3 go into 4? We usually say, "Once and one left over." But we are going to draw it to show how there can be four threes in a four!

(The accompanying drawing can be developed as the story progresses, beginning with the largest square.)

There was once a city with four walls of equal length and exactly in the middle of each wall, between each corner, there was a gate leading into and out of the city.

The ruler of this city had four sons. When they grew up, he gave them each a corner of the city between the gates. Each son built a new wall with new gates in the middle of each new wall. Now there were 4 little 3-sided cities inside of the big 4-sided city.

Each of the ruler's sons had a son. When they grew up, their grandfather gave them each a new but smaller corner of the city that was left to him. The grandsons built new walls between the gates of their fathers' cities.

Now the old ruler was left with a much smaller part of all that he used to rule but he didn't mind because his 4 sons and 4 grandsons all lived near by; and he built 2 roads crossing his part of the city so that he could easily visit his sons and grandsons, and he continued to rule over the people who lived between these two roads.

Question: How much bigger was the old ruler's whole city than the part he was left with?

Counting Corners

Yesterday we drew 12 triangles inside a square. Each triangle has 3 corners. How many corners are there in all 12 triangles?

We know: $12 \times 3 = 36$. If we didn't know it, we could work it out.

$$
\begin{array}{cccc}
12 & \text{Process:} \ 3 \times 2 = & 6 & 6 \\
\underline{\times 3} & 3 \times 10 = & 30 & \underline{+30} \\
36 & & & 36
\end{array}
$$

There are also some squares hidden in the drawing. How many? 3 squares. How many corners are there in a square? 4 corners. If 3 squares have 4 corners each, how many are "square corners?"

We know: $3 \times 4 = 12$,   *or*

$$
\begin{array}{c}
4 \\
\underline{\times 3} \\
12
\end{array}
$$

The 12 triangles make more corners than the 3 squares do. How many more?

Triangle corners:	36	
Square corners:	$-\ 12$	
	24	more corners

Which of the four processes have helped us work out the answers to these questions?

$\times$ for multiplication

$+$ for addition

$-$ for subtraction

Which process was missing? $\div$ for division

Whenever the ruler wanted to share his riches equally with his 4 sons, he had to give them away leaving less for himself. Division and subtraction both had to help. He had 10 diamonds to share with his 4 sons, keeping an equal share for himself. How?

Division divided the 10 diamonds by 5 (the father and his 4 sons).

$$10 \div 5 = 2 \qquad or \qquad 5\overline{)10}^{\,2}$$

Subtraction took 8 away and left 2.

$$10 - 8 = 2 \qquad or \qquad \begin{array}{r} 10 \\ -\ 8 \\ \hline 2 \end{array}$$

Then division divided the 8 diamonds among the 4 sons equally.

$$8 \div 4 = 2 \qquad or \qquad 4\overline{)8}^{\,2}$$

So we see that division and subtraction work well together. Multiplication and addition are the opposites of division and subtraction and they are like each other. They both do the same work of making more out of something, only multiplication does it faster.

The old ruler wanted 2 fine horses but he needed more so that his 4 sons could each have 2 fine horses also. Addition brought the horses to him, 2 at a time.

	2	for the father
	2	for the oldest son
	2	for the second son
	2	for the third son
	+ 2	for the youngest son
In all	10	fine horses in the stable

Then the ruler wanted a fine saddle for each horse and multiplication brought them to him all at once for each horseman.

$$5 \times 2 = 10 \qquad or \qquad \begin{array}{r} 2 \\ \times\, 5 \\ \hline 10 \end{array} \quad \text{fine saddles}$$

A Selection of Lessons for the Third Grade

Big Brother and Little Sister

Big Brother loved numbers. Little Sister did not. They went to the same school. He was in the fourth grade and she was in the third grade.

One night when they were in bed, they were talking before going to sleep and this is what they said:

"I just love arithmetic," said Big Brother.

"I like to read and write much better," answered Little Sister. "It's much more important."

"Oh is it?" cried Big Brother. "You couldn't do very much if you didn't know arithmetic."

"Oh yes I could," answered Little Sister. "I could get along without it very well. It doesn't do any good."

Big Brother knew better.

"Why you couldn't live even one day without arithmetic," he said. "You have to be able to count all kinds of things."

Then he told Little Sister to keep her mind on it the next day. Every time she had to use numbers she was to write it down or in some way remember what she had had to count.

The first thing the next morning their mother called, "Get up quickly, children, and hurry or you will be late to school."

Little Sister opened her eyes and looked at the clock. Both hands pointed to the number 7. Big Brother saw her looking at the clock so he jumped out of bed and brought her a pencil and a pad and made her write "clock."

At breakfast, their father was talking about their summer vacation. They were planning to rent a cabin at the beach.

"How many months vacation do you have, Little Sister?"

"Three," answered she, and Big Brother shouted!

"There! You had to count the months."

So she wrote down "months" on her pad.

Thus the day started and Little Sister wanted to prove to Big Brother that, even so, she would not have to use numbers very much; so she promised to write down all the things she had to count during the day. "But," she said, "you will see! My pad will be quite empty."

They boarded a bus. When Little Sister took out her bus pass, some pennies fell out of her purse and rolled around under the feet of other passengers. She had to look for them and pick them up. Only finding 3, she knew that she had lost 2 for she had started out with 5. When she found a seat she took out her pad and wrote "money," trying not to let Big Brother see her, for he was hidden for the moment by the crowd on the bus.

A lady on the bus noticed her writing and asked her, "What school do you go to?"

"The Rudolf Steiner School," answered Little Sister. "How many children are there in you class?" asked the lady.

"Twenty-six," answered Little Sister, then bit her tongue and took out her pad and wrote "children."

So it went through the day. When she reached home that after-noon, she showed Big Brother a page of her pad that was covered from top to bottom with words naming things she had had to count. And these were the words:

"pencils"	She thought she had lost one and counted them to make sure.
"pages"	She had been told to find page 60 in her reader and to read 3 pages.
"seasons"	The lesson had been about the seasons of the year and the teacher had asked her, "How many seasons are there?"
"stitches"	In crocheting she had to count every stitch.
"paint cups"	She had to count out cups for 5 yellows, 5 blues, 5 reds.

"steps"	In eurythmy class they had an exercise walking in a triangle, 3 steps on each side.
"sandwiches"	At lunch-time she opened her lunch box and counted the number of sandwiches her mother had put in.
"streets"	On her way home she kept watching the numbers on the street signs so as to get off at the right stop.
"houses"	When she invited a friend to come to her house to play, she had had to write the address, "262 East 95 St."
"blocks"	3 blocks from Madison Ave.

There were many other words on her pad so that when Big Brother saw it, he said, "You see? I was right. The world is so full of numbers you just have to use them to live."

Activity: Following the story, the children can write down other things they have to count every day.

Plus-Times and Minus-Divideby

Plus-Times and Minus-Divideby were not at all alike although they were brothers, Plus-Times was greedy while Minus-Divideby was very generous.

When their father died, he left them a large bag of gold pieces to share and to do with it according to what was the best in each of them.

As Plus-Times looked at the bag of gold, his eyes bulged. They got as big and as round as the bag of gold. Minus-Divideby's eyes twinkled with a light that was even brighter than the gold.

The two brothers counted the gold pieces carefully, "One for you and one for me!" until each got his fair and equal share.

Plus-Times made up his mind to use his share so as to make it grow and get bigger. He wanted to get back as much as he had shared with his brother, and even more. So this is what he did. He bought jewels, grains and furs and then sold them again for twice as much as he had paid for them. In the end he had 2 times as much gold as he had started with and it filled a bag the size of the one his father had left for both brothers.

Minus-Divideby had lots of friends. They were all very poor. One of them needed new shoes. Another needed food, Yet another had no place to live. Minus-Divideby gave them each enough of his gold to get new shoes, good food and a house to live in. He had another friend who needed a warm coat. Then there was one who could not buy milk for his baby. Another man had a leaky roof but could not pay to have it fixed. Again Minus-Divideby shared his gold so that the baby could have enough milk, a new coat could be bought to keep someone warm, and the leak in the roof could be fixed well.

All the time that Plus-Times was buying something to sell again for twice as much, Minus-Divideby was giving away and sharing his supply of gold to friends who were having one kind of trouble or another. As a result, Plus-Times became richer and richer and Minus-Divideby poorer and poorer. However, Plus-Times made no friends among those to whom he sold jewels, grain and furs and who cared only for what they could buy. They had no love for Plus-Times at all. The people who were helped by Minus-Divideby could never forget him. They smiled and waved when they saw him. They felt that the world was good because they had a friend who helped them.

At last came the day when Minus-Divideby had no gold left. He was now poorer than the friends he had helped while Plus-Times had many riches.

Now Minus-Divideby needed shoes, a warm cloak, milk for his children; and his roof leaked in a place right above his bed. He needed help and knew that his brother had much gold.

In the meantime, Plus-Times had made so much money that he did not have enough room in his house to store it. Sacks and sacks of gold filled the house from cellar to attic, leaving only a tiny closet where Plus-Times could sleep and eat and wash himself.

When Minus-Divideby came to see Plus-Times, he could barely wedge his way in through the bags of gold to the bed where Plus-Times lay like a sick man. Yes, he was really sick because he was so lonely.

Then he saw his smiling brother at his bedside, Plus-Times began to weep, crying, "No one has come to see me for a long time!"

Minus-Divideby felt so sorry for his brother that he went to the sink and found enough water to wash his brother's face and to heat up for a cup of tea. Plus-Times thought nothing had ever tasted so good. It made him feel stronger.

As the two brothers talked, they agreed that Plus-Times was rich with gold but poor in friends while Minus-Divideby was rich with friends but poor in gold.

Now, how do you think the story ends?

Did Plus-Times ever learn to give away and share?

Did Minus-Divideby ever learn to make more money than he had to begin with?

Alas, no!

To this day adding and multiplying make more of something and subtracting and dividing make less.

Perhaps Plus-Times became wise enough to let Minus-Divideby take away and share some of his gold to leave room in his house for new treasure that he could gather by selling more jewels, grains and furs at twice the price he paid for them.

Numbers Must Tell the Truth

If they are used right, numbers always tell the truth. It is not right to say $9 - 1 = 10$, or $9 \times 1 = 10$. Using 9 and 1 and 10, have them tell the truth. We are going to draw a row of 10 marbles. 9 of them are reds and the last one in the row is a blue. Then we will draw more rows under the first, each with 9 reds and 1 blue.

The truth is:

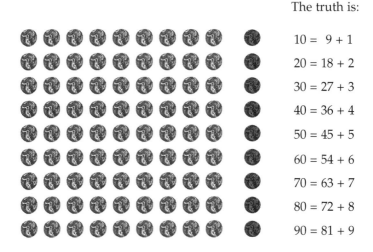

$$10 = 9 + 1$$
$$20 = 18 + 2$$
$$30 = 27 + 3$$
$$40 = 36 + 4$$
$$50 = 45 + 5$$
$$60 = 54 + 6$$
$$70 = 63 + 7$$
$$80 = 72 + 8$$
$$90 = 81 + 9$$

What number patterns do you find in the number stories?

Keeping the same numbers, change the process signs so that the stories still tell the truth.

$$10 - 9 = 1$$
$$20 - 18 = 2$$
$$30 - 27 = 3 \text{ etc. to}$$
$$90 - 81 = 9$$

Number Relationships

Children are overjoyed when they are challenged to discover "number patterns" in various kinds of progressions. They have to be guided toward significant ones if their own discoveries are superficial.

Number Endings in the Tables

The Tens: "0"

10	20	30	40	50	60	70	80	90	

The Fives: "5 0 5 0 5 0"

5	10	15	20	25	30	35	40	45	50

The Twos: "0 2 4 6 8"

0	2	4	6	8
10	12	14	16	18
20	22	24	26	28

The Eights: "0 8 6 4 2"

0	8	16	24	32
40	48	56	64	72
80	88	96	104	112

The Fours: "0 4 8 2 6"

0	4	8	12	16
20	24	28	32	36
40	44	48	52	56

The Sixes: "0 6 2 8 4"

0	6	12	18	24
30	36	42	48	54
60	66	72	78	84

The Threes: "0   3   6   9
               2   5   8
               1   4   7"

0	3	6	9	12	15	18	21	24	27
30	33	36	39	42	45	48	51	54	57
60	63	66	69	72	75	78	81	84	87

The Sevens: "0   7   4   1
               8   5   2
               9   6   3"

0	7	14	21	28	35	42	49	56	63
70	77	84	91	98	105	112	119	126	133

The Ones: "0   1   2   3   4   5   6   7   8   9"

0	1	2	3	4	5	6	7	8	9
10	11	12	13	14	15	16	17	18	19

The Nines: "0   9   8   7   6   5   4   3   2   1"

0	9	18	27	36	45	54	63	72	81
90	99	108	117	126	135	144	153	162	171

Subtractions

10 − 8 = 2	8 − 5 = 3	7 − 2 = 5
20 − 16 = 4	16 − 10 = 6	14 − 4 = 10
30 − 24 = 6	24 − 15 = 9	21 − 6 = 15
40 − 32 = 8	32 − 20 = 12	28 − 8 = 20
50 − 40 = 10	40 − 25 = 15	35 − 10 = 25
60 − 48 = 12	48 − 30 = 18	42 − 12 = 30
etc.	etc.	etc.

Additions

3 + 2 = 5	4 + 3 = 7	9 + 1 = 10
6 + 4 = 10	8 + 6 = 14	18 + 2 = 20
9 + 6 = 15	12 + 9 = 21	27 + 3 = 30
12 + 8 = 20	16 + 12 = 28	36 + 4 = 40
etc.	etc.	etc.

Counting Exercises

Starting with 1 add 5:

1	6
11	16
21	26
31	36 etc.

Starting with 2 add 5:

2	7
12	17
22	27
32	37 etc.

As they become more difficult, they can be worked out in writing before practiced orally.

Starting with 1 add 4:

1	5	9	13	17
21	25	29	33	37
41	45	49	53	57
		etc.		

Starting with 2 add 4:

2	6	10	14	18
22	26	30	34	38
42	46	50	54	58
		etc.		

Starting with 1 add 4:

1	5	9	13	17
21	25	29	33	37
41	45	49	53	57
		etc.		

Starting with 2 add 4:

2	6	10	14	18
22	26	30	34	38
42	46	50	54	58
		etc.		

Starting with 1 add 2:   (the odd numbers!)

1	3	5	7	9	11
11	13	15	17	19
21	23	25	27	29
		etc.		

Starting with 1 add 3:

1	4	7	10	13	16	19	22	25	28
31	34	37	40	43	46	49	52	55	58
61	64	67	70	73	76	79	82	85	88
		etc.						

Early Measures

From the Columbia Encyclopedia

Long distances by land or sea were measured by the day's journey. "Ten-Sleep Lake," named by Native Americans, measured maybe its length, or the distance around it.

The size of a field that a man with a yoke of oxen could plow in one day was a furrow-long (furlong), and its width that of four yoked oxen abreast, or 1 rod (about 16 ft.).

1 pace was 3 ft., 1 mile was 1000 paces.

Four oxen in their stalls were allowed 16 ft. of stall space. 16 ft. is still a standard length of boards.

The ft. was the length of a man's foot. The hand was the width of a man's hand (4 inches).

The yard was the length of a step, or the distance from the nose to the finger-tips.

The fathom was from finger-tips to finger-tips of the outstretched arms (6 ft.).

The inch was the outer joint of the thumb, or the length of 3 grains of barley placed end to end.

In Everything There Lieth Measure
—Chaucer

After reviewing linear measure in a practical way, the children can be asked, "What other things can be measured besides lengths?" One can take up their suggestions but direct them to ways of measuring liquids, "dry" bulks, weights and time. The following are possible introductions to these various measures. They should be then taken up in practice problems that can be related to their own experience in a useful way.

Liquid Measure

Do we measure water or milk in inches and feet?

Three different children can be asked to pour 3 inches of water into 3 differently sized containers; then pour each 3 inches into three (of the same size) glass or plastic drinking cups to see that each cup will contain a different amount of water.

Now fill a gallon jug with water and pour the water into four quart bottles. Pour the water from one quart into 2 pint bottles. Pour from the pint into 2 cups.

As one demonstrates, the names of the various measures are given and the table of Liquid Measure is written on the blackboard:

1 gallon	=	4 quarts
1 quart	=	2 pints
1 pint	=	2 cups

Questions for the children to write and work out:

1 gal.	=	? pts.
1 qt.	=	? c.
1 gal.	=	? c.
3 gal. milk	=	? c.
$\frac{1}{2}$ gal. milk	=	qts.
$2\frac{1}{2}$ gal. milk	=	? qts. = ? pts. = ? c.

Dry Measure

Show the class, if possible, a bushel basket, a peck, a half-peck, a quart (berry) basket and a pint basket.

Question:	"How many gallons of milk would this biggest basket hold?"
Answer:	"It wouldn't hold any milk because it would all run out through the slats."
Question:	"Where have you seen such baskets?"
Answer:	"In roadside garden markets."
Question:	"What is in the baskets?"
Answers:	"Potatoes."
	"Apples."
	"Peaches."
	"Berries." etc.

These baskets are dry measures. Fruits and vegetables will not leak out of them.

Stand the baskets in a row from the largest to the smallest and have the children judge and compare them as to size and what they will hold. For instance, how many of the smallest of them would be enough to fill the largest with, say, raspberries? Would you want to fill this huge basket with raspberries? Why not? What would happen to the berries at the bottom of this basket? Would the same thing happen to potatoes or apples?

The names of these dry measures are only partly different from the names of liquid measures. The largest is the *bushel*, the next largest is the *peck*, then comes the *half-peck*. The two smaller are the quart and the *pint*.

Through questioning and judging, the Table of Dry Measure is written on the blackboard and copied.

1 bushel (bu.)	=	4 pecks (pk.)
1 peck	=	8 quarts
1 quart	=	2 pints

Weights

Going back to Linear Measure, the teacher can measure and mark, with tapes and names on a wall, the height of each child in the class.

Then could come the question, "Since John and Donald are exactly the same height, in what way are they different?"

Then if it's acclaimed that John is fat and Donald skinny, ask, "Would anyone be apt to say that John is wider than Donald?"

"Heavier?"

Here we come to measuring differences in size by means of weighing. John and Donald could now be weighed on the school scale.

Before the following discussion, the class should be shown an apothecary's scale or balance and experience what happens when various objects are weighed against each other.

In how many different ways do we weigh things?

We can weigh things with our two hands and find out which is heavier. Inwardly we can weigh what we like against what we don't like, what we want to do against what we ought to do: wanting to play against having to do homework, giving something to another against keeping it for oneself, letting someone else go first instead of pushing ahead ourselves.

What is balance?

"All work and no play makes Jack a dull boy."

"Do unto others as you would have them do unto you."

To give thanks for what we receive, or to forgive someone.

Human beings are not valued according to the number of pounds they weigh but for the kind of people they are. Then we weigh material things, we judge their value and give something in return for it. In a store the value is given in money. The value of a good man cannot be exchanged for money.

In ancient Egypt, the land of the Pharaohs, it was said that when a man died, he had to stand before Osiris, the god of Light, and have his heart weighed in the scales of justice. In those scales every man's heart was weighed against the feather of truth. If it was lighter than the feather, then the man could be admitted into the land of the gods. If it was heavier, then the man was condemned to the dark underworld where the light of the sun was unknown.

We didn't weigh John and Donald against the feather of truth. They are still very much alive and were weighed with their shoes on. The scale measured their weights in *pounds*.

There are various systems of weights throughout the world. In the United States we use the following one:

1 ton (tn.)	=	2000 (lb.)
1 pound	=	16 ounces (oz.)
1 ounce	=	16 drams

If we weigh a human being in pounds, in what would we weigh his handkerchief? What would be the most useful measure of weight for an elephant? For a postage stamp? Can any of you answer these questions:

2 pounds	=	? ounces
2 ounces	=	? drams

$$3 \text{ tons} = ? \text{ pounds}$$
$$1 \text{ ton} = ? \text{ ounces}$$

Time

Riddle

It has a round-round face
With arms in the nose's place.
  The long arm runs fast,
  The short comes in last
  But it's not a real race.
  Each one keeps its pace
To tell you the time.
What is it?

A very small boy was once asked, "What time do you get up in the morning?"

His answer was, "Sometimes I get up when the clock is up, sometimes I get up when the clock is down."

Of course this little boy had not even started school yet and couldn't read the numbers on the face of the clock. What are the numbers? 1 through 12. How are the spaces between the numbers divided? Into fives. How many spaces are there? $12 \times 5 = 60$.

If you will watch the clock's arms (hands), you will see that the long one goes through all 60 spaces while the short one goes through 5. Sometimes there is a third arm, as long as the other long one but very thin, that goes through all 60 spaces while the long one goes through only one.

Who can still say the time rhyme you learned in Second Grade:

Sixty seconds make a minute.
Put a lot of kindness in it.
Sixty minutes make an hour.
Work with all your might and power.

Which of the hands do you think points to the hour? Which points to the minutes? What does the fastest of the three hands mark off as it ticks around the face?

Measures of Time (to write)

1 hour	=	60 minutes
1 minute	=	60 seconds
1 hour	=	? seconds
		(and similar questions)

A Selection of Lessons for the Fourth Grade

The Numbers Workers: An introduction to carrying and borrowing

Have you ever known anyone whose last name was Carpenter or Mason or Miner or Cook? Such names probably came from long ago when an ancestor was a carpenter or a mason or a miner or a cook. The names came from the kind of work a man did. I am going to tell you a story about four brothers whose last name was Numbers because they worked with numbers. Their first names explain the kind of work they did.

And these were their names:

> Add Numbers
> Multiply Numbers
> Divide Numbers
> Subtract Numbers

The first three brothers were very successful in their work. Add and Multiply liked to collect things. They had many collections; stamps, broken glass, nails, bottles, marbles; and their pockets were always full. Add liked to make piles and piles of the things he had collected until there was hardly any space in his room for him to come and go. Multiply was even worse for he tried to get two or three or four or five times as much as anyone else in his collections. Add and Multiply were always carrying numbers of things from place to place. The neighbors said, "What a family! They have so many places to put things, and carry them back and forth all day long, never resting."

Even Divide Numbers did a lot of carrying but he was different from Add and Multiply. He was always sharing his treasures, dividing them into smaller piles and carrying them to his friends in some other place. If there was anything left over he would carry that to a new place.

Subtract Numbers was indeed very different from the other three Numbers workers. He might pick up some pebbles or some bottle tops and put them in his pockets but the pockets had holes in them. He kept losing his treasures and never had as much as he'd start off with. If the neighbors saw a trail of bottle caps, or bits of string, or nuts and bolts, or broken springs scattered along the street, they would say, "Subtract Numbers has been this way."

One could hardly say that Subtract ever carried anything but he did borrow a lot, for he would go to the other Numbers to borrow what he needed.

When we add or multiply numbers we have to know how to carry over from one number place to the next starting with the ones' place. We carry from the ones to the tens, from the tens to the hundreds, from the hundreds to the thousands, ever upward and to the left.

Examples:

$$
\begin{array}{r}
{\scriptstyle 1}\\
42\\
35\\
+\,85\\
\hline
162
\end{array}
\qquad
\begin{array}{r}
{\scriptstyle 1}\\
2486\\
+\,1605\\
\hline
4091
\end{array}
\qquad
\begin{array}{r}
{\scriptstyle 11111111\ 11111}\\
596742381026479\\
+\,107689869095631\\
\hline
704432250122110
\end{array}
$$

(adding after multiplying)

$$
\begin{array}{r}
{\scriptstyle 1}\\
34\\
\times\,4\\
\hline
136
\end{array}
\qquad
\begin{array}{r}
{\scriptstyle 31}\\
263\\
\times\,5\\
\hline
1315
\end{array}
\qquad
\begin{array}{r}
{\scriptstyle 2}\\
3018\\
\times\,3\\
\hline
9054
\end{array}
\qquad
\begin{array}{r}
{\scriptstyle 22}\\
489\\
\times\,3\\
\hline
1467
\end{array}
\qquad
\begin{array}{r}
{\scriptstyle 1112222}\\
123456789\\
\times\qquad\ 3\\
\hline
370370367
\end{array}
$$

When we divide numbers we start with the highest number place and carry ever downward and to the right to the ones.

Examples:

$$
\begin{array}{r}
122\\
6\,\overline{)732}\\
{\scriptstyle 1\,1}
\end{array}
\qquad
\begin{array}{r}
13\\
4\,\overline{)52}\\
{\scriptstyle 1}
\end{array}
\qquad
\begin{array}{r}
115\\
3\,\overline{)345}\\
{\scriptstyle 1}
\end{array}
$$

$$
\begin{array}{r}
1975308642\\
5\,\overline{)9876543210}\\
{\scriptstyle 4321\ 4321}
\end{array}
$$

In subtracting, we start with the ones' place and work to the tens, borrowing as we go. How much do we borrow?

Examples:

$$
\begin{array}{r}
\overset{1}{2}2 \\
-13 \\
\hline 9
\end{array}
\qquad
\begin{array}{r}
\overset{1}{4}2 \\
-16 \\
\hline 26
\end{array}
\qquad
\begin{array}{r}
2\overset{1}{3}5 \\
-106 \\
\hline 129
\end{array}
\qquad
\begin{array}{r}
2\overset{111}{3}54 \\
-1365 \\
\hline 989
\end{array}
\qquad
\begin{array}{r}
9876\overset{11111}{5}4321 \\
-864197532 \\
\hline 123456789
\end{array}
$$

Can you explain why we do not always have to carry or borrow?

Riddle

What is it
that you cannot see,
or hear,
or smell,
or taste,
or touch,
yet—you can't
get dressed without it,
eat breakfast without it,
get to school without it,
learn your lessons without it,
have recess without it,
get home without it,
play without it,
have supper without it,
get to bed without it
or sleep without it?

You cannot measure it in inches or feet,
in gallons or quarts,
in pounds or ounces.
But it is a great treasure
which you *can* measure!

What is it?

(Time)

Area Measure

Suggestion: Too Much Land, *the story by Leo Tolstoy, can be told before introducing area measure.*

Was the farmer, in the story I told, interested in the distance around the land or was he interested in the amount of land within the borders? We would call the land inside the "area."

To determine an area we have to have a surface measure instead of a line measure. If we wanted to paint the blackboards in the school, we would have to find out how much paint we'd need. Every can of paint, no matter what size, has printed directions on it as to how much surface it will cover. How would you measure the whole surface of the blackboard in this room?

Give each child a square paper and have him measure each edge with his ruler to find that it is 1 foot long.

Now each of you has a "square foot" and that is square measure. It could be a square inch or a square yard or a square mile. Square measures are uses for measuring surface areas. Let us see how many times a square foot fits into the area of this blackboard. (This should be done very carefully, with the help of chalk marks.)

We find that the blackboard is 4 feet high and 6 feet long. There are 4 rows with 6 squares in each row. How many squares in all? $4 \times 6 = 24$. So the surface area of the blackboard is 24 square feet. We could also say that the blackboard is 4 squares high and 6 squares long.

Note: Have the children measure various surfaces in the room, a door, a window, a table top or such, using their foot squares to find out "about how many square feet" are in each surface.

Next step or lessons

From a blackboard drawing showing an area 6 sq. ft. (2 rows of 3 squares) one can ask, "How many ways can we count the square feet in an area?" (Square feet often has the abbreviation sq. ft.)

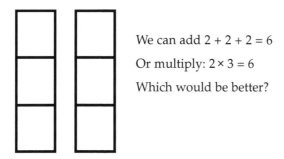

We can add 2 + 2 + 2 = 6

Or multiply: 2 × 3 = 6

Which would be better?

Suppose you wanted to find the area of a wall that is 35 ft. long by 15 ft. high? Would you have to use a piece of paper or of wood that is a foot square and keep laying it down to mark off the square feet? That would really be childish!

You know that each side of a square foot measures 1 linear foot. In the blackboard drawing the width measures 2 linear feet and the length or height measures 3 linear feet.

2 ft. x 3 ft. = 6 sq. ft.

You could find the area of the wall in the same way. What would you multiply?

$$\begin{array}{r} 35 \\ \times\ 15 \\ \hline 175 \\ +\ 35\ \\ \hline 525\ \text{sq. ft.} \end{array}$$

The rule is: We find an area by multiplying the length by the width.

Now let us add another row of 3 square feet to the two on the board. It makes a larger area that is 3 feet long on each side. What is the measure of the area? 9 sq. ft.

3 ft. x 3 ft.= 9 sq. ft.

Since 3 ft. = 1 yard, we can call the area 1 square yard.

1 yd. x 1 yd. = 1 sq. yd.

Assignment

Mark off 12 inches on each side of your 1 sq. ft. paper (measure) to get the right number of square inches in a square foot. If you know what 12 x 12 is, you will know the correct number of square inches that should appear in your drawing.

A Further Question

Now that you know that there are 144 square inches in 1 sq. ft., can you figure cut how many sq. in. there are in 1 sq. yd.? Can you find three ways of doing it?

I.   Nine square feet would be 9×144 sq. in.

II. If 1 yd. measures 36 inches, the number of sq. in. in a sq. yd.

III. Or you could add 144 sq. in. nine times!

Which would you find to be the easiest way? Try all three and see if you get the same answer each time.

Table of Square Measure

1 square yard = 9 sq. ft.

1 square foot = 144 sq. in.

Someday you will learn the area of 1 square mile!

The Fraction Tree

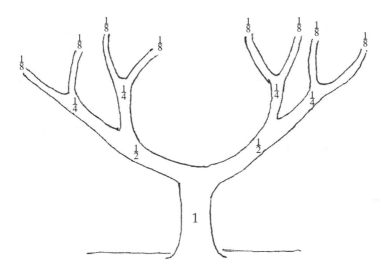

The branches get smaller and smaller, the more there are.

Have an Apple!
Introduction to fractions

Melinda came to school with an apple. She was just about to eat it when Christopher arrived and saw it, She wouldn't keep it all to herself so she cut it into two pieces and gave half of the apple to Christopher. Just then Jeanne and Ralph came in. Melinda and Christopher cut their halves in half. At that time the apple was in 4 pieces. Each person had one fourth. Before they could eat the fourths, Donald, Lisa, John, and Linda came in. Now the fourths were cut in two and there were eight pieces for eight children. The apple had been divided into eighths that were about to be gobbled up when Claude, Francis, Erich, Olivia, Miriam, Max, Michaela, and Hillary burst into the room. Now they had to cut each of the eight pieces of apple in two, to make sixteen pieces, very tiny, each piece being one sixteenth of the apple. They were all so small.

Before, there was one piece. Now there were sixteen pieces; but though 16 is a larger number than 1, each piece was smaller, by far, than the 1 apple.

Rather than eat the little sixteenths, the children could have put them all together again, with sugar and flour and perhaps a few more apples, to make an apple pie.

This is an apple pie. To share the pie, first cut it into 2 equal pieces:

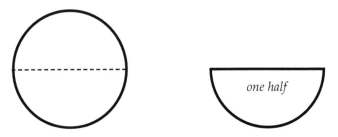

Each piece is one half a pie.

As the 2 halves of the pie make one whole, they are related to the whole by the number 2 but we have to allow that 1 is divided into 2 pieces.

What would be a good way to show that in writing?

We can use the knife-cut line as a divider line and if we write it, it could read "1 divided by 2" or "one half."

$$\frac{1}{2}$$

A part of a number is called a '"fraction" of it. We can call the divider line the "fraction line."

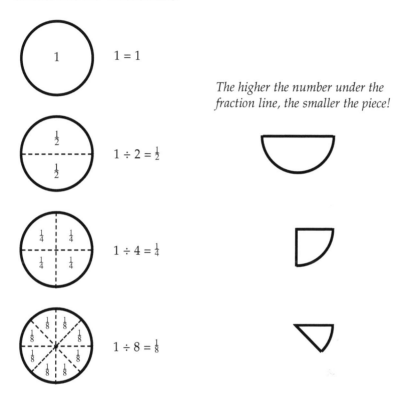

$1 = 1$

The higher the number under the fraction line, the smaller the piece!

$1 \div 2 = \frac{1}{2}$

$1 \div 4 = \frac{1}{4}$

$1 \div 8 = \frac{1}{8}$

Number and Name

Here are two words to remember: numerator and denominator. What other word does number make you think of? I'll give a hint. There is just one letter missing. Could it be the letter "b"? The other word is number. Who knows what language "nom" comes from and what it means? Could it be French and does it mean name? Just so!

The number above the fraction line is called the numerator and it gives us the number of fraction-parts that are named below the fraction line in the denominator. If we have divided something into eighths, 5 of those eighths would be written as $\frac{5}{8}$.

$$\underset{8}{\overset{5}{—}}$$

Numerator   This is the number that counts the parts.

Denominator   This is the name of the parts, or fraction.

Adding Fractions

The blueberries were ripe and the children went berry-picking. They each carried a 2-pound can. I'm afraid they ate more than they collected because at the end of an hour Jimmy had only $\frac{1}{3}$ of a pound in his can and Jill had only $\frac{1}{3}$ of a pound in hers. How many thirds had they all together?

$$\frac{1}{3} + \frac{1}{3} = \frac{2}{3}$$

What part of the fraction did we add? The numerator! The denominator remained the same. Can you add the following fractions in the same way?

$$\frac{2}{7} + \frac{3}{7} = ? \qquad \frac{5}{16} + \frac{5}{16} = ? \qquad \frac{7}{10} + \frac{2}{10} = ? \qquad \text{etc.}$$

Subtracting Fractions

In October, the apples were ripe and the children went apple-picking with their father. While he picked 1 whole bushel of apples, the two of them only filled $\frac{2}{3}$ of a bushel. How much less did they pick? 1 whole is the same as $\frac{3}{3}$.

$$\frac{3}{3} - \frac{2}{3} = \frac{1}{3}$$

What part of the fraction did we subtract? The numerator! We subtracted in thirds. It was like subtracting 2/apples from 3/apples, leaving 1/apple. Can you subtract other fractions?

$$\frac{4}{5} - \frac{1}{5} = ? \qquad \frac{5}{8} - \frac{2}{8} = ? \qquad \frac{10}{10} - \frac{4}{10} = ? \qquad \text{etc.}$$

Fractions of Numbers Greater than 1

So far we have learned to divide 1 whole into fractions of the whole:

$$\tfrac{1}{12} \text{ of 1 year} = 1 \text{ month}$$
$$\tfrac{1}{12} \text{ of 1 foot} = 1 \text{ inch}$$
$$\tfrac{1}{4} \text{ of 1 gallon} = 1 \text{ quart}$$

We can also divide numbers larger than 1 into their "fraction-parts".

$$2\overline{)12}^{\,6}$$

means 12 divided into 2 equal parts is 6, in each part,

or $\tfrac{1}{2}$ of 12 = 6

To find $\tfrac{1}{2}$ of a number we divide it by 2.

To find $\tfrac{1}{3}$ of a number we divide it by ?

To find $\tfrac{1}{4}$ of a number we divide it by ?

Practice work

$\tfrac{1}{2}$ of 10	$\tfrac{1}{4}$ of 16
$\tfrac{1}{5}$ of 10	$\tfrac{1}{3}$ of 21
$\tfrac{1}{6}$ of 18	$\tfrac{1}{7}$ of 49
$\tfrac{1}{8}$ of 56	$\tfrac{1}{9}$ of 54
$\tfrac{1}{10}$ of 100	

If $\tfrac{1}{2}$ of 12 is 6, then $\tfrac{1}{2}$ a year is 6 months.
If $\tfrac{1}{2}$ of 24 is 12, then $\tfrac{1}{2}$ a day is 12 hours.

$\tfrac{1}{3}$ of a year is ? months
$\tfrac{1}{6}$ of an hour is ? minutes
$\tfrac{1}{7}$ of a week is ? days
$\tfrac{1}{12}$ of a minute is ? seconds

$\frac{1}{4}$ of a bushel is ? pecks
$\frac{1}{8}$ of a peck is ? quarts
$\frac{1}{2}$ of a quart is ? pints
$\frac{1}{4}$ of of 2 bushels is ? pecks   etc.

Fractions of Odd Numbers

Lisa's mother told her that she and Melinda and Linda could have all the cookies left in the cookie jar. They found 7 cookies in the jar. They divided them so that each girl got 2 cookies and there was one left over; so they divided that into 3 equal parts. What did each girl get?

$$3\overline{)7}^{\,2\frac{1}{3}}$$

Ralph, Donald, Claude and Max divided 13 sticks of candy so that they each had 4 and there was 1 left over. This they divided into 4 equal pieces. What did each boy get?

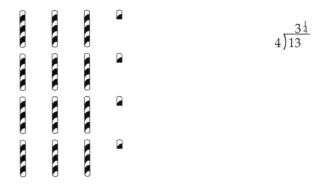

$$4\overline{)13}^{\,3\frac{1}{4}}$$

What do you notice about the *remainder* in the answer?

It can become the numerator of a fraction. What number is the denominator of the fraction?

Suppose we wanted to divide 11 apples among 4 children? How would we figure out each one's equal share?

$$4 \overline{)11} \; \; 2\tfrac{3}{4}$$

Practice Work

$$2 \overline{)19}^{?} \qquad\qquad 3 \overline{)13}^{?}$$

$$5 \overline{)17}^{?} \qquad\qquad 3 \overline{)25}^{?} \qquad \text{etc.}$$

Multiplying with Fractions

Note: This should be taken up after the class is thoroughly familiar with adding and subtracting fractions, maybe toward the end of the year.

Two of a Kind

When I say, "two of a kind," I might mean 2 robins, or 2 garnets, or 2 daisies, or two always-happy children. If I say, "2 of 1," I do mean 2 × 1. 3 of 1 is the same as 3 × 1. Likewise 6 of 12 is 6 × 12. If 1 of 5 means 1 × 5, then $\frac{1}{5}$ of 5 means $\frac{1}{5}$ × 5.

Oral Practice Before Writing

$\frac{1}{5} \times 5 = \frac{1}{5}$ of $5 = 1$ $\frac{2}{5} \times 5 = \frac{2}{5}$ of $5 = 2$

$\frac{1}{3} \times 3 = \frac{1}{3}$ of $3 = 1$ $\frac{2}{7} \times 7 = \frac{2}{7}$ of $7 = 2$

$\frac{1}{4} \times 4 = \frac{1}{4}$ of $4 = 1$ etc. $\frac{2}{9} \times 9 = \frac{2}{9}$ of $9 = 2$ etc.

Now we have some harder questions: How would we figure out:

$$\tfrac{1}{5} \text{ of } \tfrac{1}{5} \quad \text{or}$$
$$\tfrac{2}{9} \text{ of } \tfrac{1}{9} \quad \text{or}$$
$$\tfrac{3}{7} \text{ of } \tfrac{4}{7} \quad ?$$

Drawing

Have the children draw, with their rulers, a rectangle 3 inches wide and 12 inches long, then cut it out for folding.

1. Fold it into 2 equal parts. $(2 \times \tfrac{1}{2})$
2. Fold into 4 equal parts. $(\tfrac{4}{4})$
3. Fold into 8 equal parts. $(\tfrac{8}{8})$

Which is larger, $\tfrac{1}{2}$ or $\tfrac{1}{4}$, $\tfrac{1}{4}$ or $\tfrac{1}{8}$?

Writing

(Referring to their folded rectangle)

$$\tfrac{1}{2} = \tfrac{?}{4} \qquad\qquad \tfrac{4}{8} = \tfrac{?}{2}$$
$$\tfrac{1}{2} = \tfrac{?}{8} \qquad\qquad \tfrac{6}{8} = \tfrac{?}{4}$$
$$\tfrac{2}{4} = \tfrac{?}{2} \qquad\qquad \tfrac{3}{4} = \tfrac{?}{8}$$
$$\tfrac{4}{8} = \tfrac{?}{4}$$

$$\tfrac{1}{2} \text{ of } \tfrac{1}{2} = ?$$
$$\tfrac{1}{2} \text{ of } \tfrac{1}{4} = ?$$
$$\tfrac{1}{4} \text{ of } \tfrac{4}{8} = ?$$
$$\tfrac{1}{4} \text{ of } \tfrac{1}{2} = ?$$

These are all fractions of fractions, or fractions times fractions. From now on, when we see the times-sign ($\times$), we can remember that it means "of."

Use the times-sign ($\times$) and refer to folded rectangle if necessary.

$$\tfrac{1}{2} \times \tfrac{1}{2} = \tfrac{1}{4}$$
$$\tfrac{1}{2} \times \tfrac{1}{4} = \tfrac{1}{8}$$

Could you use the times-sign above the fraction line to multiply the numerators, and below the fraction line to multiply the denominators? (Yes.)

$$\frac{1 \times 1 = 1}{2 \times 2 = 4}$$

$$\frac{1 \times 1 = 1}{2 \times 4 = 8}$$

In the same way, multiply:

$$\tfrac{1}{2} \times \tfrac{1}{3}$$
$$\tfrac{1}{2} \times \tfrac{1}{5}$$
$$\tfrac{1}{2} \times \tfrac{1}{6}$$

Imagine a chocolate bar divided into 9 equal pieces. (Drawing on board.) What part of the whole bar is 1 piece? What part of it are 3 pieces?

$$\tfrac{1}{3} \times 9 = 3$$
$$\tfrac{1}{3} \times 3 = 1$$
$$\tfrac{1}{3} \times 1 = \tfrac{1}{3}$$
$$\tfrac{1}{3} \times \tfrac{1}{3} = \tfrac{1}{9}$$

We can see all this in the drawing. What else can we see?

$$1 = \tfrac{9}{9} \qquad\qquad \tfrac{2}{3} = \tfrac{6}{9}$$
$$\tfrac{1}{3} = \tfrac{9}{9} \qquad\qquad \tfrac{1}{3} = \tfrac{?}{9}$$

We cannot see $\tfrac{1}{2}$ of the chocolate bar in 9ths because 9 is an odd number and 2 does not divide into it evenly.

But there is a way to find $\tfrac{1}{2}$ of $\tfrac{9}{9}$. How?

$$\frac{1 \times 9 = 9}{2 \times 9 = 18}$$

What did we do? We multiplied the numerator by the numerator, 1 × 9, and the denominator by the denominator, 2 × 9. That is the rule for multiplying fractions. Using this rule, do the following examples:

Practice Work
(oral, then written)

$$\tfrac{2}{3} \times \tfrac{1}{2} = \tfrac{2}{6}$$
$$\tfrac{3}{4} \times \tfrac{4}{5} = \tfrac{12}{20}$$
$$\tfrac{1}{3} \times \tfrac{4}{7} = \tfrac{4}{21}$$
$$\tfrac{2}{5} \times \tfrac{1}{2} = \tfrac{2}{10}$$

Simplest Terms of Fractions

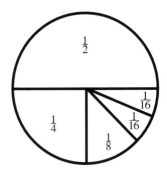

The *fraction story* of this circle could be written as:

1 whole $= \tfrac{1}{1} = \tfrac{2}{2} = \tfrac{4}{4} = \tfrac{8}{8} = \tfrac{16}{16}$.

Which of these five fractions would be the simplest to use?

We can see that $\tfrac{2}{16} = \tfrac{1}{8}$
$\tfrac{2}{8} = \tfrac{1}{4}$
$\tfrac{2}{4} = \tfrac{1}{2}$
$\tfrac{2}{2} = \tfrac{1}{1}$ or 1

If I asked you to multiply $\frac{8}{8}$ times $\frac{16}{16}$, what would you do to make it easier? Could you change both to their simplest terms, before you multiply? And would you get 1 × 1 = 1?

Changing a fraction to its simplest terms is called "reducing" the fraction.

In the following fractions, what part of the denominator is the numerator?

$$\frac{4}{8} \qquad \rightarrow \quad 4 \text{ is } \frac{1}{2} \text{ of } 8$$

$$\frac{5}{10}$$

$$\frac{3}{9}$$

$$\frac{6}{9}$$

$$\frac{4}{6}$$

$$\frac{4}{12}$$

$$\frac{8}{10}$$

It was easy to recognize that 3 goes into 9 3 times so that we could reduce $\frac{4}{4}$ to $\frac{1}{3}$. What we really thought was "3 divided by 3 = 1" and "9 divided by 3 = 3." We divided both the numerator and the denominator by 3, and changed the fraction to $\frac{1}{3}$.

These are the two ways of reducing fractions to their simplest terms:

1. to ask what part of the denominator is the numerator,

2. to divide the numerator and the denominator by some number that goes into both.

Practice Work—Oral and Written
Reduce the first way: $\frac{4}{24}$, $\frac{6}{36}$, $\frac{4}{20}$, $\frac{9}{18}$, $\frac{10}{100}$, etc.

Reduce the second way: $\frac{6}{8}$, $\frac{9}{12}$, $\frac{10}{15}$, $\frac{15}{20}$, $\frac{12}{16}$, etc.

(There are some fractions that cannot be reduced. Why not? $\frac{8}{9}$, $\frac{7}{16}$, $\frac{4}{3}$, $\frac{11}{13}$, etc.)

Question

If you reduce $\frac{16}{24}$ to $\frac{8}{12}$, have you reduced it to its simplest terms? Not yet. You can go further, and should.

$$\frac{16}{24} = \frac{8}{12} = \frac{2}{3}$$

As long as there is a number that goes into both numerator and denominator, a fraction can still be simplified. When there is no such number, you have to stop.

Expanding Fractions

When we reduce a fraction to its lowest terms, we come to a stop; but we can expand it again and never come to a stop!

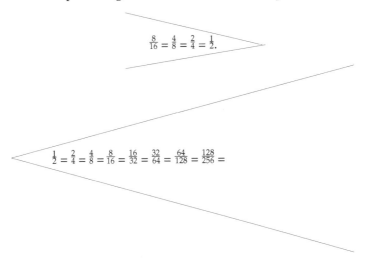

$$\frac{8}{16} = \frac{4}{8} = \frac{2}{4} = \frac{1}{2}.$$

$$\frac{1}{2} = \frac{2}{4} = \frac{4}{8} = \frac{8}{16} = \frac{16}{32} = \frac{32}{64} = \frac{64}{128} = \frac{128}{256} =$$

It is good that we can do this. We know that in order to add or subtract fractions we add or subtract just the numerators.

$$\frac{5}{8} - \frac{3}{8} = \frac{2}{8}$$

$$\frac{7}{9} - \frac{5}{9} = \frac{2}{9} \quad \text{etc.}$$

What do you notice about the denominators? In each example they are the same.

Imagine that you have a bowl of fruit, a mixture of pears and apples. You cannot subtract or add the apples and the pears unless you give them a common *name* such as *fruit*. You can say, "7/fruits minus 3/fruits equals 4/fruits." Just so, fractions have to have a common denominator (name) before they can be added or subtracted. You can arrive at a common denominator by either reducing or expanding certain of the fractions.

Finding the Common Denominator

(Working through examples like these, have the children either reduce or expand a fraction where necessary to find the common denominator. Begin to have them reduce answers to their simplest terms.)

$$\frac{1}{2} + \frac{1}{4} = \frac{2}{4} + \frac{1}{4} = \frac{3}{4}$$

$$\frac{4}{6} + \frac{1}{3} = \frac{2}{3} + \frac{1}{3} = \frac{3}{3} = 1$$

$$\frac{4}{6} - \frac{1}{3} = \frac{2}{3} - \frac{1}{3} = \frac{1}{3}$$

$$\frac{6}{8} - \frac{1}{2} = \frac{6}{8} - \frac{4}{8} = \frac{2}{8} = \frac{1}{4}$$

$$\frac{10}{16} + \frac{1}{8} = \frac{5}{8} + \frac{1}{8} = \frac{6}{8} = \frac{3}{4} \quad \text{etc.}$$

Proper Fractions, Improper Fractions, Mixed Numbers

If $\frac{8}{8} = 1$, what is $\frac{9}{8}$? It is $\frac{1}{8}$ more than 1. We must change it to $1\frac{1}{8}$. We call a fraction wherein the numerator is larger than the denominator an "improper" fraction. It is improper to call it simply a fraction because it is more than 1 whole. It is a fraction more. How would you change $\frac{10}{8}$ to get a mixed number? Remember to reduce the fraction to its simplest terms. $\frac{10}{8} = 1\frac{2}{8} = 1\frac{1}{4}$.

Practice work—oral, then written

If $\frac{5}{5} = 1$, $\frac{7}{5} = ?$, $\frac{9}{5} = ?$, $\frac{10}{5} = ?$

If $\frac{3}{3} = 1$, $\frac{5}{3} = ?$, $\frac{4}{3} = ?$, $\frac{6}{3} = ?$, $\frac{7}{3} = ?$

Change from improper fractions to mixed numbers:

$$\frac{5}{2}, \frac{7}{4}, \frac{9}{4}, \frac{10}{6}, \frac{14}{6}$$

Change from mixed numbers to improper fraction:

$$3\tfrac{1}{3}\, , 5\tfrac{1}{2}\, , 7\tfrac{1}{3}\, , 3\tfrac{1}{4}\, , 10\tfrac{1}{3}\, , 4\tfrac{1}{2}$$

Studies in Square Numbers
(done in a fourth grade)

Counting and stepping, up and back, forward and backward

Stamp: 1
Step: 1 <u>2</u> 1
                           1 2 <u>3</u> 2 1
                        1 2 3 <u>4</u> 3 2 1
                     1 2 3 4 <u>5</u> 4 3 2 1
                  1 2 3 4 5 <u>6</u> 5 4 3 2 1
               1 2 3 4 5 6 <u>7</u> 6 5 4 3 2 1
            1 2 3 4 5 6 7 <u>8</u> 7 6 5 4 3 2 1
         1 2 3 4 5 6 7 8 <u>9</u> 8 7 6 5 4 3 2 1
      1 2 3 4 5 6 7 8 9 <u>10</u> 9 8 7 6 5 4 3 2 1

(This active exercise can be practiced toward the beginning of a lesson for several days before any question or further study of it is introduced.)

First Study—written

$$1 = 1$$
$$1 + 2 + 1 = 4$$
$$1 + 2 + 3 + 2 + 1 = 9$$
$$1 + 2 + 3 + 4 + 3 + 2 + 1 = 16$$
$$1 + 2 + 3 + 4 + 5 + 4 + 3 + 2 + 1 = 25$$
$$1 + 2 + 3 + 4 + 5 + 6 + 5 + 4 + 3 + 2 + 1 = 36$$
$$1 + 2 + 3 + 4 + 5 + 6 + 7 + 6 + 5 + 4 + 3 + 2 + 1 = 49$$

etc. to 100

It should become apparent that the numbers "at the top of the hill" are the squared numbers.

Second study—oral practice and written

The Square Table

$1 = 1 \times 1$
$4 = 2 \times 2$
$9 = 3 \times 3$
$16 = 4 \times 4$
$25 = 5 \times 5$
$36 = 6 \times 6$
$49 = 7 \times 7$
$64 = 8 \times 8$ etc.

The Tens as Helpers

Some of you may remember the line from a number rhyme you learned in First Grade:

"Five toes on each foot help me balance and stand." That is, altogether, ten toes. We also have ten fingers. And they certainly help in many another way, especially in playing the piano or the harp. These 2 tens are a part of our physical bodies.

$2 \times 10 = 20$, and 20   is a multiple of 10.
4×10 is a multiple of 10.
50×10 is a multiple of 10.

Tens and the Multiples of Ten can be Helpers in adding, subtracting, multiplying and dividing any set of numbers. Do you think there is any connection between the helpfulness of our ten fingers in counting and using 10 as a helper with other numbers?

What are the multiples of 10 up to 100?

10 20 30 40 50 60 70 80 90 100,   as easy as counting by ones!

Before we can use the tens as helpers, we need to be sure how the ones are combined to make ten. Can you guess how many combinations there are? We can work it out on this Number Wheel:

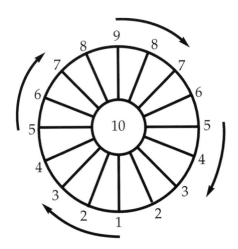

Starting with 9 and reading the numbers, with their opposites, in the direction that the arrows point to, we find the combinations are:

9 + 1	4 + 6
8 + 2	3 + 7
7 + 3	2 + 8
6 + 4	1 + 9
5 + 5	

From 9 + 1 to 5 + 5, there are 5 combinations with the others as opposites of the same numbers.

Knowing the combinations in 10 helps us to think out other numbers:

since   6 from 10 is 4
6 from 20 is 14
6 from 50 is 44

70 – 6 = ?	10 – 3 = ?	10 – 9 = ?
60 – 6 = ?	20 – 3 = ?	20 – 9 = ?
40 – 6 = ?	50 – 3 = ?	80 – 9 = ?

Harder numbers become easier if we remember the tens:

$$50 - 12 = 50 - 10 - 2 = 40 - 2 = 38$$
$$70 - 15 = 70 - 10 - 5 = 60 - 5 = 55$$
$$60 - 14 = ?$$
$$40 - 17 = ?$$
$$30 - 18 = ?$$
$$90 - 19 = ?$$
$$80 - 13 = ?$$

or

$$50 + 12 = 50 + 10 + 2 = 60 + 2 = 62$$
$$60 + 16 = ?$$
$$40 + 15 = ?$$
$$30 + 19 = ?$$
$$70 + 14 = ? \qquad\qquad \text{etc.}$$

How would you think out 50 – 22 ?

$$50 - 22 = 50 - 20 - 2 = 30 - 2 = 28$$
$$70 - 36 = ?$$
$$80 - 54 = ?$$
$$80 - 82 = ?$$

What would you think to add 43 and 21? To subtract?

$$
\begin{array}{r}
40 + 20 = \ 60 \\
3 + \ \ 1 = \underline{+ 4} \\
64
\end{array}
\qquad\qquad
\begin{array}{r}
40 - 20 = \ 20 \\
3 - \ \ 1 = \underline{+ 2} \\
22
\end{array}
$$

or $\quad 43 - 20 - 1 = 22$

Practice

Add and Subtract the following pairs of numbers:

$$65 \ \ 38 \ \ 54 \ \ 19 \ \ 24 \ \ 35 \ \ 42 \ \ 68$$
$$44 \ \ 22 \ \ 32 \ \ 16 \ \ 13 \ \ 24 \ \ 34 \ \ 31$$

Just as we need to know the five combinations of numbers 1 through 9 that make 10, we need to know the combinations that add up to numbers greater than 10. Start with 9.

add:	9	9	9	9	9	9	9	9
	2	3	4	5	6	7	8	9

add:	8	8	8	8	8	8
	3	4	5	6	7	8

7	7	7	7
4	5	6	7

add:	6	6
	5	6

So, here we have 20 combinations and together with their opposites there are 36. How is that? They are called the 36 Number Facts in Addition.

Let us work out some number facts in Subtraction and see how many there are.

9	9	9	9	9	9	9	9	9	9
0	1	2	3	4	5	6	7	8	9
9	8	7	6	5	4	3	2	1	0

8	8	8	8	8	8	8	8	8
0	1	2	3	4	5	6	7	8
8	7	6	5	4	3	2	1	0

7	7	7	7	7	7	7	7
0	1	2	3	4	5	6	7
7	6	5	4	3	2	1	0

6	6	6	6	6	6	6
0	1	2	3	4	5	6
6	5	4	3	2	1	0

5	5	5	5	5	5
0	1	2	3	4	5
5	4	3	2	1	0

4	4	4	4	4
0	1	2	3	4
4	3	2	1	0

3	3	3	3
0	1	2	3
3	2	1	0

2	2	2
0	1	2
2	1	0

1	1
0	1
1	0

We have 54 Subtraction Facts but not so hard to remember because we have already learned a lot of number combinations.

Practice in using 10 (oral and written);

$$11 - 7 = 10 - 7 + 1 \qquad\qquad 11 + 7 = 10 + 7 + 1$$
$$15 - 6 = 10 - 6 + 5 \qquad\qquad 15 + 6 = 10 + 6 + 5$$
$$13 - 8 = 10 - 8 + 3 \qquad\qquad 13 + 8 = 10 + 8 + 3$$
$$16 - 7 = 10 - 7 + 6 \qquad\qquad 16 + 7 = 8 + 10 + 7$$

Starting with the tens, add:

11 + 12	11 + 14	11 + 16	11 + 18	11 + 15	12 + 13
12 + 14	12 + 17	13 + 13	13 + 15	14 + 14	14 + 15
15 + 15	14 + 16	13 + 17	12 + 18	11 + 19	15 + 17
13 + 18	16 + 18	17 + 16	19 + 14	12 + 19	13 + 17
13 + 18	22 + 39	33 + 29	45 + 37	54 + 39	63 + 29
44 + 38	75 + 26	53 + 28	etc.		

When we get into the hundreds, we can use them to help us add or subtract just as we have the tens and multiples of ten:

Example

$$201 + 308 = 200 + 300 + 1 + 8 = 500 + 9 = 509$$

Mental practice:
306 + 407, 209 + 306, 408 + 305, 708 + 207, 405 + 506, etc.

Multiplying and dividing, helped by the tens
Those of you who know your Times Tables will find it easy to do this.

2×46 is $(2 \times 40) + (2 \times 6)$ or $80 + 12$ or $90 + 2$ which is 92

Do some others in the same way:

$3 \times 35, 4 \times 24, 3 \times 16, 2 \times 37$, and so on.

If 6 is 2×3, or 6 divided by 3 is 2, then

6 tens divided by 3 tens is 2. $30\overline{)60}$ is 2.

$300\overline{)600}$ is 2, etc.

Do these divisions in your heads:

$20\overline{)80}$ $30\overline{)90}$ $40\overline{)120}$ $50\overline{)150}$ $70\overline{)560}$
                                                                                                etc.

Long Division
Review or introduce the terms used in dividing:

$$\text{divisor}\overline{)\text{dividend}}^{\text{quotient}}$$

Usually the fastest way to figure something out is by thinking. However we have to be able to show how we think in writing, and sometimes the writing helps us in thinking.

If I ask you to divide 56 by 4, you can do so without writing it down. You can think 10×4 is 40 and 16 left over; 16 is 4×4; 10 ($\times$ 4) and 4 ($\times$ 4) is 14×4.

So $4\overline{)56}^{14}$

Or, you can think it the way you write it. 4 into 5 is 1 and 1 remainder; carry the 1 (as a 10) and add the 6 to make 16; 4 into 16 is 4. The quotient (14) is written above the dividend.

Divide (at the board):

$$6\overline{)84} \qquad\qquad 8\overline{)96}$$

showing what you "carry."

In these divisions we do not show every "thinking step" in writing. We can take time to do that in what is called "long division." In long division we place the quotient above the dividend:

$$\begin{array}{r} 14 \\ 4\overline{)56} \end{array} \qquad \text{and how do we think it up there?}$$

$$\begin{array}{r} 14 \\ 4\overline{)56} \\ \underline{4} \\ 16 \\ \underline{16} \\ 00 \end{array}$$

4 into 5 goes once, or is 1;	*divide*
1 × is 4;	*multiply*
4 from 5 is 1;	*subtract*
bring down 6;	*bring down*
4 into 16 is 4;	*again divide*
4 × 4 is 16;	*multiply*
16 from 16 is zero	*subtract*

Here is a song to help you remember what to do:

Di – vide, Mul – ti – ply, Sub – tract, bring – down.

You can see why this is called long division. We do not need to divide the long way when there is only one figure in the divisor; but if there are 2 or more figures in the divisor, long division helps us because we do not have to keep all the numbers in our heads.

Practice work in long division at the board and then in note books using tens or multiples of tens as a help in dividing:

$17\overline{)510}$ 17 does not go into 5 but it
will go into 51.
20 goes into 50 at least 2 times.
$2 \times 17 = 34$
$51 - 34 = 17.$
So, 17 will go into 51 3 times, and
into 0 zero times.

Mr. Jones, the chicken farmer, sold 3744 eggs to the market. He packed them by the dozen in egg boxes. How many boxes did he use?

$12\overline{)3744}$

These 3744 eggs were laid by 72 hens. If each laid the same number of eggs, how many did each lay?

$72\overline{)3744}$ etc.

A Selection of Lessons for the Fifth Grade

History of Numbers

(Excerpts from *Numbers and Numerals* by Smith and Ginsburg, Bureau of Publications, Teachers College, Columbia Univ.)

For *one*, all known people have used **l** , the raised finger,

                       or **—** , a stick laid down,

                       or **O** , a pebble.

For *two*, **ll** , two fingers,   or **=** , two sticks,

When rapidly written, **ll** became **Ν** , from which came **Γ** used by the Arabs and Persians. The **=**, rapidly became **Ζ** written, which developed into our 2.

The cuneiform numerals used about 5000 years ago by the Sumerians and the Chaldeans, and later by the Babylonians and Assyrians, were stamped on clay tablets by sticks which were usually triangular with sharp edges but also circular.

Υ = 1   **ΥΥ** = 2   **ΥΥΥ** = 3   or

D = 1   **O** = 10   **D** = 60   **DO** = 60 + 10

In the Far East, **≡** was 3. The most common form in China and Japan even today is **≡**. These three lines joined together as **3** became our 3. **lll** rapidly formed the Persian and Arabic **Γ**. Turned on its side it became the Sanskrit **ʒ** .

The *four*, also developed from the arrangement of sticks or fingers, was **ΥΥΥΥ** in Babylonia, **llll** in Egypt and Rome. The Arabs joined the four lines in **Σ** and it appears today as **ع** .

The Number 27,529 was written like this by the Early Egyptians.

The Story of Pythagoras

(References: Richards Encyclopedia; *History of Math*, Vol.10; Encyclopedia Brittanica; *The Great Initiates* by Edouard Schure.)

In ancient Greece, the Father of the Gods had the name of Zeus. There is an old, old story that Zeus wanted to find the very center of the earth so he started two eagles in their flight from east and west and they met at a certain place in Greece where there rose a circle of rugged mountains and amongst them a deep gorge. From within the gorge rose a high rock, surrounded by precipices. Here the eagles met, here was the center of the world. Here the Greeks built a temple to Apollo, the son of Zeus and the God of Light. Behind the temple there was a cleft in the rocks from which there came a vapory mist and, above the cleft, there sat a priestess who was called the Pythoness. As the mist rose up around her, she was able to see into the future and speak of things that would happen some day. Many people would come to this place, Delphi, to ask questions about the future.

One day, a wealthy jeweler and his young wife came to Delphi to consult the Pythoness. She told them that they would have a son "who would be useful to all men throughout all time."

When the child was born, the parents were filled with great joy; and when he was a year old, his mother took him to a priest who blessed him so that he would be wise and good when he grew up.

The name of the boy was Pythagoras and he grew to be gentle, calm and thoughtful. From his eyes there shone a light as of great wisdom, even as a small boy, and his parents saw to it that he had the wisest of teachers.

As Pythagoras grew older and began to think for himself, he found that his teachers did not all tell him the same thing. One teacher declared that all life arises from the earth and its elements, only to return to it again; and that human beings were prisoners of the earth and of nature; and that although they couldn't do anything except to suffer and endure the laws of nature, they could try to understand and know them. Another of the teachers said that all life comes from the heaven of the gods and that human beings on earth must pray to the gods that they might soon return to heaven.

One starry night, when Pythagoras was eighteen years old, he went to a hilltop above the city where he lived. He could see the lights of the King's palace among the twinkles of other lights. He could see the harbor and the lights of ships from other lands, and above him the stars beamed forth their light. He heard the shouts and songs of wild merry-makers in the palace, then the shrieks of slaves, men who were being sold into slavery because they had disobeyed the king. They were being whipped with nail-studded thongs to make them board the slave ships.

Then a great question arose in the soul of Pythagoras. If the earth was man's prison and if to reach heaven man had to pray to the gods and if, between heaven above and earth below, stood the human being in pain, in suffering and even madness, why does the human being exist? Thereafter this question would not leave him.

To find the answer he made up his mind to go to Egypt. The temples there were schools where priests taught the answers to such questions. He stayed for 22 years in Egypt and studied what were called "the sacred numbers." Then, from Babylon, there came a great army and the Egyptian temple was destroyed. Pythagoras was taken, as a prisoner, to Babylon and kept there for 12 years. Yet, there too he found wise teachers. From them he learned about the stars and their movements.

Much wisdom became his and, when he became free to leave Babylon, he went back to Greece, to Delphi, there to teach the priests of the temple such great knowledge that they, who had been getting to say a lot of meaningless words, could again give wisdom to the people.

After a year he went to Crotona, a Greek town in Italy. There he started a school to which many young men and women came in search of learning.

Any new pupils in the school of Pythagoras would be expected to remain silent for a period of at least 2 years, maybe 5, and mainly listen to their instructors without discussion or argument. Such a pupil would even be locked up, alone, in a bare room and given a slate and water and dry bread until he could find the answer to such a question as this: "What is the meaning of a triangle inscribed within a circle?"

When the pupil was brought out of the "test" room and led into a room full of older students, they would make fun of him as they had been instructed to do by their teachers. Hungry, tired, and having no idea what a triangle inscribed in a circle meant, and hearing the older students beg him to tell them what he had discovered, the new pupil showed what kind of a person he was. If he lost his temper, broke his slate, cursed the school and its teachers and walked out, nobody stopped him. If, on the other hand, he would answer that he had much yet to learn and would be willing to try such a test again and again, even a hundred times over, in order to gain a bit of wisdom, he would be welcomed as a worthy student in the school.

Pythagoras cared more for what kind of a person his pupil was than whether or not the pupil could discover the meaning of a triangle inscribed within a circle. But if he could do this, so much the better.

What were some of the teachings of Pythagoras?

He taught about the Music of the Spheres, music of such exquisite sweetness as man has ever known, that sounded forth as the heavenly bodies wheeled around a great, central fire from which they got their light. He discovered and taught about the harmonic intervals which underlie the production of musical sounds and that the length of a musical string is in exact mathematical relation to the height of its tone.

He taught that "all things are numbers," because he found truth in numbers and used them as a key to understanding the laws of nature. He taught that the whole world was formed through different combinations of numbers. One combination made a stone, another made a virtue such as human kindness. Just as there are 10 Heavenly Spheres revolving around Hestia, the central Fire, to make the Music of the Spheres, so there are 10 opposites in the union from which the universe arises:

1   the limited and the unlimited

2   the odd and the even

3   the one and the many

4   the right and the left

5   the male and the female

6   rest and motion

7   the straight and the curved

8   light and darkness

9   good and evil

10 square and oblong

He taught that the elements of numbers are the *odd* and the *even*. When the odd is divided in two equal parts, a unit is left over in the middle: (oo) o (oo). When the even is so divided, an empty field is left over without a master and without a number, showing that it is defective and incomplete: (oo)   (oo). The first even number (2) is feminine, the first odd number (3) is masculine, and the union of 2 + 3, or 5, is marriage. Number 4, the first square number, is justice.

Pythagoras also discovered the numbers that lie hidden in various shapes, for instance in the triangle, square and oblong. He called them "triangular numbers," "square numbers" and "oblong numbers."

The *triangle numbers* arise through adding 1 + 2 + 3 + 4 and so on because they can be pictured as triangles. The number 10 is the triangle of 4, as shown below:

```
            o
         o     o
      o     o     o
   o     o     o     o
```

The *square numbers* appear when, starting with 1, we add successive odd numbers: 1 + 3 + 5 + 7 and so on. They can be pictured as forming ever larger squares:

```
o x # o x #
x x # o x #
# # # o x #        36 is the square of ?
o o o o x #
x x x x x #
# # # # # #
```

The *oblong numbers* can take the shape of an oblong when we add successive even numbers: 2 + 4 + 6 + 8, etc.

```
o o x o x o x
x x x o x o x
o o o o x o x
x x x x x o x
o o o o o o x
x x x x x x x
```

If we count the number of figures in each new oblong, we see that they are multiples of one even number and one odd number: 1×2, 2×3, 3×4, and so on.

Pythagoras esteemed arithmetic above all things, lifted it up from just service of commerce and made it the basis of the order in this world. Yet, he introduced weights and measures for the use of men engaged in commerce. He explored and discovered many relationships in geometry which even you will learn about in your school life today.

Pythagoras was an ancient man, yet his wisdom is a part of modern thought and knowledge. As the Pythoness had foretold, this thinker has been "useful to all men throughout all time."

Chart of Equivalent Fractions in One Inch

$$\frac{1}{16} \quad \frac{1}{8} \quad \frac{3}{16} \quad \frac{1}{4} \quad \frac{5}{16} \quad \frac{3}{8} \quad \frac{7}{16} \quad \frac{1}{2} \quad \frac{9}{16} \quad \frac{5}{8} \quad \frac{11}{16} \quad \frac{3}{4} \quad \frac{13}{16} \quad \frac{7}{8} \quad \frac{15}{16} \quad 1$$

$$\frac{2}{16} \qquad \frac{4}{16} \qquad \frac{6}{16} \qquad \frac{8}{16} \qquad \frac{10}{16} \qquad \frac{12}{16} \qquad \frac{14}{16} \qquad \frac{16}{16}$$

$$\frac{2}{8} \qquad\qquad \frac{4}{8} \qquad\qquad \frac{6}{8} \qquad\qquad \frac{8}{8}$$

$$\frac{2}{2} \qquad\qquad\qquad\qquad \frac{4}{4}$$

We have counted and compared the fractions that show on our rulers within one inch. We find that $\frac{1}{8}$ is the same as $\frac{2}{16}$, is the same as $\frac{4}{16}$ and $\frac{2}{8}$, and so on.

By studying the chart we have made, can you tell which of the equal, or equivalent fractions (that is, fractions that have equal value) have been expanded and which have been reduced?

Let's work it out:

Expanded Fractions   *Reduced Fractions*

$$\frac{1}{8} < \frac{2}{16} \qquad\qquad \frac{4}{16} > \frac{2}{8}$$

$$\frac{1}{4} < \frac{4}{16} \qquad\qquad \frac{8}{16} > \frac{4}{8}$$

$$\frac{3}{8} < \frac{6}{16} \qquad\qquad \frac{12}{16} > \frac{6}{8}$$

$$\frac{1}{2} < \frac{8}{16} \qquad\qquad \frac{16}{16} > \frac{8}{8}$$

$$\frac{5}{8} < \frac{10}{16} \qquad \text{etc.}$$

What process do we use to expand fractions? (multiplication)

What process do we use to reduce fractions? (division)

What numbers do we multiply or divide by? In each pair of fractions there is a single multiplier or a single divisor. If we compare the numerators and the denominators, we can discover the secret number which you may not be able to see and which operates on both.

In expanding $\frac{1}{2}$ to $\frac{8}{16}$ the secret multiplier is 8.

$$\frac{8 \times 1}{8 \times 2} = \frac{8}{16}$$

In reducing $\frac{12}{16}$ to $\frac{6}{8}$ the secret divisor is 2.

$$2\overline{)12} = 6$$
$$2\overline{)16} = 8$$

The rule to follow is: When we expand or reduce a fraction we must multiply or divide both parts of the fraction by the same number.

There's no end to expanding any fraction. Can you find the secret multipliers in:

$$\frac{2}{3} = \frac{4}{6} = \frac{20}{30} = \frac{40}{60} = \frac{120}{180}$$

When reducing fractions we often come to a stop because there is no divisor that will go into both the numerator and the denominator of that fraction. Then we say we have reduced it to its lowest terms. To find out about this, try reducing the following fractions until you cannot do it any more. You can use 2 as the divisor.

$$\frac{20}{20} \qquad \frac{16}{20} \qquad \frac{12}{20} \qquad \frac{8}{20} = \frac{4}{20}$$

Dividing with Fractions

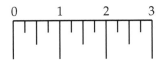

Three Questions

How many $\frac{1}{2}$ inches are there in 1 inch?   2.

How many times does $\frac{1}{2}$" go into 1"?   2 times.

What is 1 divided by $\frac{1}{2}$"?   2.

If $2 \times \frac{1}{2}$" = 1"   then $1" \div \frac{1}{2}" = 2$

      $4 \times \frac{1}{2}$" = 2"   then $2" \div \frac{1}{2}" = 4$

Complete the following

$6 \times \frac{1}{2}$" =   then $3" \div \frac{1}{2}" =$

$2 \times \frac{1}{4}$" =   then $\frac{1}{2}" \div \frac{1}{4}" =$

$3 \times \frac{1}{4}$" =   then $\frac{3}{4}" \div \frac{1}{4}" =$

$4 \times \frac{1}{4}$" =   then $1" \div \frac{1}{4}" =$

$8 \times \frac{1}{4}$" =   then $2" \div \frac{1}{4}" =$

$12 \times \frac{1}{4}$" =   then $3" \div \frac{1}{4}" =$

Dividing by $\frac{1}{2}$ is not the same as dividing by 2. When we cut a chocolate cake into 2 equal parts, each part is $\frac{1}{2}$ of the cake.

Dividing by 2 is to find $\frac{1}{2}$ of something.

Dividing by 3 is to find $\frac{1}{3}$ of something.

Dividing by 4 or 5 is to find $\frac{1}{4}$ or $\frac{1}{5}$ of something. So, if that something is a fraction, it works like this:

$$\frac{1}{2} \div 2 \text{ means } \frac{1}{2} \text{ of } \frac{1}{2}, \qquad \text{or } \frac{1}{2} \times \frac{1}{2}$$
$$\frac{1}{4} \div 2 = \qquad \text{or } \frac{1}{2} \times \frac{1}{4}$$
$$\frac{1}{2} \div 4 = \qquad \text{or } \frac{1}{4} \times \frac{1}{2}$$

What has changed? Division has been changed to multiplication. Some other matter has also been changed.

What disappeared when we changed from division to multiplication? The whole numbers! 2 became $\frac{1}{2}$, 4 became $\frac{1}{4}$. And what is the rule for multiplying fractions? Multiply the numerators by the numerators and the denominators by the denominators. Does it matter which fraction comes first?

$$\frac{1}{2} \times \frac{1}{4} = \frac{1}{8} \text{ is the same as } \frac{1}{4} \times \frac{1}{2} = \frac{1}{8}$$

To come to the rule for dividing with fractions we need to remember one more thing, and that is that we can write whole numbers as fractions:

$$\frac{1}{1} \quad \frac{2}{1} \quad \frac{3}{1} \quad \frac{4}{1} \quad \frac{5}{1} \quad \frac{6}{1} \quad \frac{7}{1} \quad \text{etc.}$$

$$\frac{1}{4} \div \frac{5}{1} \text{ means } \left(\frac{1}{5} \text{ of } \frac{1}{4} \right) \text{ or } \left(\frac{1}{5} \times \frac{1}{4} \right) \text{ or } \frac{1}{5} \times \frac{1}{4}$$

Leaving out the two middle steps, we can write:

$$\frac{1}{4} \div \frac{5}{1} = \frac{1}{4} \times \frac{1}{5} = \frac{1}{20}$$

$$\frac{1}{6} \div \frac{3}{1} = \frac{1}{6} \times \frac{1}{3} = \frac{1}{18}$$

$$\frac{1}{3} \div \frac{4}{1} = \frac{1}{3} \times \frac{1}{4} = \frac{1}{12}$$

What have we done each time? We inverted (turned upside down) the divisor and multiplier. Follow this rule with some other examples:

$$\frac{1}{2} \div \frac{3}{4} = \frac{1}{2} \times \frac{4}{3} = \frac{4}{6} = \frac{2}{3} \text{ reduced to lowest terms}$$

$$\frac{3}{4} \div \frac{1}{2} = \frac{3}{4} \times \frac{2}{1} = \frac{6}{4} = \frac{3}{2} = 1\frac{1}{2}$$

You Can Cancel It

How many times have you heard that a game or a picnic has been canceled because of rain? Have you ever canceled a dentist appointment because you had a bad cold? Such occasions are simply "crossed off" your planned calendar, In work with fractions we can cancel certain numbers but it is not like canceling picnics or appointments that aren't there any more (except when they are postponed). In fractions another number takes the place of the one you cancel.

By now you know well enough that $\frac{4}{8}$ can be reduced to $\frac{1}{2}$, that $\frac{2}{6}$ can be reduced to $\frac{1}{3}$, and so on. When you reduce $\frac{4}{8}$ to $\frac{1}{2}$, you have divided both 4 and 8 by 4. You have done it in your mind. But you can do it very quickly in writing too. The number 4 is called the "common factor," which you divide into the numerator and the denominator of $\frac{4}{8}$. In writing you cross off the numerator and put 1 above it, you cross off the denominator and put 2 below it, You are canceling one number and putting another in its place.

4 is the common factor $\dfrac{\overset{1}{\cancel{4}}}{\underset{2}{\cancel{8}}} = \dfrac{1}{2}$ *and 4 is the largest number you can use that will go into both 4 and 8*

Other examples

Using the largest common factor you can, simplify or reduce the following fractions, showing how to cancel:

$$(2)\ \frac{\overset{2}{\cancel{4}}}{\underset{5}{\cancel{10}}} \qquad (2)\ \frac{\overset{3}{\cancel{6}}}{\underset{4}{\cancel{8}}} \qquad (2)\ \frac{\overset{5}{\cancel{10}}}{\underset{6}{\cancel{12}}} \qquad (3)\ \frac{\overset{2}{\cancel{6}}}{\underset{3}{\cancel{9}}} \qquad (5)\ \frac{\overset{2}{\cancel{10}}}{\underset{3}{\cancel{15}}} \qquad (6)\ \frac{\overset{2}{\cancel{12}}}{\underset{3}{\cancel{18}}} \qquad (7)\ \frac{\overset{1}{\cancel{7}}}{\underset{4}{\cancel{28}}}$$

Suppose you have to find out what $\frac{3}{4}$ of $\frac{5}{6}$ of a yard of red ribbon is.

One way

$$\frac{3}{4} \times \frac{5}{6} = \frac{\overset{5}{\cancel{15}}}{\underset{8}{\cancel{24}}} = \frac{5}{8} \quad \textit{of a yard.}$$

Now, instead of canceling and reducing in the answer, can you do it in the multiplicand or the multiplier? Not in $\frac{3}{4}$ and not in $\frac{5}{6}$, not without first doing something else.

We can write all the numerators above a single fraction line and put all denominators under it:

$$\frac{3 \times 5}{4 \times 6} = \frac{15}{24}$$

You know that in multiplying you can change the right numbers around:

$$\frac{5 \times 3}{4 \times 6} = \frac{15}{24}$$

Now you can cancel in the multiplicand:

$$\frac{5 \times \overset{1}{\cancel{3}}}{4 \times \underset{2}{\cancel{6}}} = \frac{5}{8}$$

But why change any numbers around? It wouldn't make any difference to leave them where they were in the first place. You can still find which ones to cancel!

$$\frac{\overset{1}{\cancel{3}}}{4} \times \frac{5}{\underset{2}{\cancel{6}}} = \frac{1}{4} \times \frac{5}{2} = \frac{5}{8}$$

Cancel as many fractions as you can before multiplying:

$$\frac{\overset{1}{\cancel{2}} \times \overset{1}{\cancel{14}} \times \overset{1}{\cancel{5}} \times \overset{1}{\cancel{6}}}{\underset{1}{\cancel{7}} \times \underset{3}{\cancel{15}} \times \underset{4}{\cancel{8}} \times \underset{5}{\cancel{10}}} = \frac{1 \times 1 \times 1 \times 1}{1 \times 1 \times 2 \times 5} = \frac{1}{10}$$

The Decimal System

The word *decimal* comes from the Greek word *deka*, meaning ten. December was the tenth month of the early Roman calendar which began the year in March. A decade is a period of ten years. A decapod is a crab or a lobster with ten feet. A decagon is a ten-sided figure. The American system of money is based on decimals, or multiples of 10. Our number places in counting are based on multiples of 10.

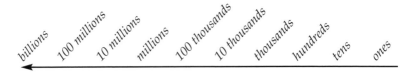

As we move from right to left, from the ones to the millions, with each move we multiply by 10. What happens when we move in the opposite direction? We are dividing by 10.

We can keep moving to the right, beyond the ones place but we put a point between the ones and the places that follow to show that they are decimal fractions.

tenths   hundredths   thousandths   10 thousandths   100 thousandths   millionths   10 millionths   100 millionths   billionths

What is the difference between 9.0 and 0.9? Which of you would be richer if one if one had $9.0 and the other had $.90?

Whole numbers get larger as they move to the left of the decimal point. Fractions get smaller as they move to the right of the point.

× 10			× 100	
900 .	9000 .		90 .	9000 .
90 .	900 .		9 .	900 .
9 .	90 .		.9	90 .
.9	9 .		.09	9 .
.09	.9		.009	.9
.009	.09		.0009	.09
.0009	.009		.00009	.009

÷ 10			÷ 100	
900 .	90 .		90.	00.9
90 .	9 .		9.0	0.09
9 .	.9		.9	.009
.9	.09		.09	.0009
.09	.009		.009	.00009
.009	.0009		.0009	.000009
.0009	.00009		.00009	.0000009

How far can you read fractions?

Common Fractions and Decimal Fractions

If I ask, "What is the easiest multiplication table?" you would answer, "The one-table." The next easiest is the ten-table. All you have to do is multiply by 1 and add a zero to the answer: $1 \times 12 = 12$, and $10 \times 12 = 120$. Next in easiness is the 100-table. $100 \times 12 = 1200$. And so it goes through the thousands, 10-thousands, 100-thousands, 1-millions and up. We just have to keep track of the number of zeros in the multiplier. For instance:

$$99 = 1 \times 99 \qquad 990 = 10 \times 99 \qquad 9900 = 100 \times 99 \qquad 99000 = 1000 \times 99$$

Which of these fractions of a dollar can you change to cents most quickly?

$$\tfrac{1}{5} \qquad \tfrac{1}{3} \qquad \tfrac{1}{2} \qquad \tfrac{1}{20} \qquad \tfrac{1}{4} \qquad \tfrac{1}{10} \qquad \tfrac{1}{100} \qquad \tfrac{1}{7} \qquad \tfrac{1}{12}$$

Which is easier to think out?

12 + 25 *or* 10 + 20	46 – 7 *or* 40 – 10
21 × 32 *or* 20 × 30	650 ÷ 36 *or* 600 ÷ 30

Which is easier to add?

$$6\tfrac{5}{16} \text{ inches} + 4\tfrac{3}{8} \text{ inches}$$

or 6.312 inches + 4. 375 inches

Suppose you had to measure something as accurately as possible down to the width of a hair. The smallest space on your rulers is $\tfrac{1}{16}$ inch. The width of a hair is much smaller. There are measuring instruments called calipers that can be used to measure hair-like parts. If you wanted to measure parts or fractions of $\tfrac{1}{16}$ of an inch, it would go something like this: (Have class work out these examples.)

$$\tfrac{1}{2} \times \tfrac{1}{16} = \tfrac{1}{32}$$
$$\tfrac{1}{2} \times \tfrac{1}{32} = \tfrac{1}{64}$$
$$\tfrac{1}{2} \times \tfrac{1}{64} = \tfrac{1}{128}$$
$$\tfrac{1}{16} \times \tfrac{1}{16} = \tfrac{1}{256}$$
$$\tfrac{1}{32} \times \tfrac{1}{16} = \tfrac{1}{512}$$
$$\tfrac{1}{64} \times \tfrac{1}{16} = \tfrac{1}{1024}$$

$\tfrac{1}{1024}$ of an inch is about $\tfrac{1}{1000}$ of an inch.

Wouldn't it be simpler if your inch was divided into 10ths rather than 16ths? How would that read?

$$\tfrac{1}{2} \times \tfrac{1}{10} = \tfrac{1}{20}$$
$$\tfrac{1}{2} \times \tfrac{1}{20} = \tfrac{1}{40}$$
$$\tfrac{1}{10} \times \tfrac{1}{10} = \tfrac{1}{100}$$
$$\tfrac{1}{10} \times \tfrac{1}{100} = \tfrac{1}{1000}$$

Just as it is easier to answer number questions by using the tens, it is simpler to use 10ths and 100ths than to use 16ths and 36ths and other common fractions.

We divide a yard into 3rds to get feet, or into 36ths to get inches. We divide feet into 12ths to get inches and divide inches by multiples of 2 such as 4ths, 8ths, and 16ths.

In Europe the measure closest to a yard is a meter. It is divided into 10ths to get a decimeter which is again divided into 10ths to get a centimeter. One centimeter divided by 10 is a millimeter. Can you say quickly what part a millimeter is of a meter? $10 \times 10 \times 10 = ?$ or $\frac{1}{10} \times \frac{1}{10} \times \frac{1}{10} = ?$ Can you tell me as quickly what part of a yard $\frac{1}{16}$ of an inch is?

Where are 10ths, 100ths and 1000ths used other than in the European metric system?

> Automobile odometers.
>
> Rain gauges, which measure every 100th of an inch.
>
> American money.
>
> Thermometers.

These are some uses of the decimal system.

When we write $\frac{1}{10}$, we are writing it as a common fraction. We change it to a decimal fraction when we drop the denominator and change the fraction line to a decimal point as .1

$$\frac{5}{10} = .5 \qquad\qquad \frac{12}{100} = .12$$
$$\frac{6}{10} = .6 \qquad\qquad \frac{25}{100} = .25 \qquad \text{etc.}$$

Decimal fractions are fractions that can only be in 10ths, 100ths, 1000ths, and so on. They appear in their proper places to the right of the decimal point. Can you read these decimal fractions correctly:

> .1
> .01
> .001
> .0001
> .00001
> .000001
> .0000001

Knowing these number places is enough if you want to change 10ths or millionths from common fractions to decimal fractions. We have to do something more if we want to change, or "reduce," other common fractions to decimal fractions.

$\frac{1}{10}$ means 1 divided by 10, or $10\overline{)1}$, and if we extend the dividend with the help of a decimal point, we can get enough number places to divide 1 by 10:

$$10\overline{)1.0}$$

but we have to show the quotient as a fraction, a *decimal fraction*. There has to be a decimal point in the quotient right above the one in the dividend.

$$10\overline{)1.0}^{\,0.1}$$

Practice Worked through in Class

$\frac{1}{2} = 2\overline{)1.0}^{\,0.5}$ $\qquad$ $\frac{1}{4} = 4\overline{)1.00}^{\,0.25}$

$\frac{1}{5} = 5\overline{)1.0}^{\,0.2}$ $\qquad$ $\frac{1}{25} = 25\overline{)1.00}^{\,0.04}$

By this time we can see that we are dividing the numerator by the denominator each time we change a common fraction to a decimal fraction. Follow the rule and do some more.

$\frac{2}{5} = 5\overline{)2.0}^{\,0.4}$ $\qquad\qquad$ $\frac{3}{5} = 5\overline{)3.0}^{\,0.6}$

$$\frac{3}{20} = 20\overline{)3.00}^{\,0.15} \qquad\qquad \frac{9}{20} = 20\overline{)9.00}^{\,0.45}$$
$$\begin{array}{r} 3.0 \\ \hline 1\,00 \\ \underline{1\,00} \end{array} \qquad\qquad \begin{array}{r} 8.0 \\ \hline 1\,00 \\ \underline{1\,00} \end{array}$$

Class or Home Assignment

Reduce these common fractions to decimal fractions;

$$\frac{3}{4} \qquad \frac{6}{10} \qquad \frac{7}{10} \qquad \frac{4}{5} \qquad \frac{3}{25} \qquad \frac{6}{25} \qquad \frac{8}{20} \qquad \frac{3}{8} \qquad \frac{2}{3}$$

A Table of Fractions and their Decimal Equivalents worked through to the second decimal place with fractional remainders—to be memorized.

$$1 \text{ whole} = 1.00$$

$$\tfrac{1}{2} = .50$$

$$\tfrac{1}{3} = .33\tfrac{1}{3}$$

$$\tfrac{1}{4} = .25$$

$$\tfrac{1}{5} = .20$$

$$\tfrac{1}{6} = .16\tfrac{2}{3}$$

$$\tfrac{1}{7} = .14\tfrac{2}{7}$$

$$\tfrac{1}{8} = .125 \ or \ .12\tfrac{1}{2}$$

$$\tfrac{1}{9} = .11\tfrac{1}{9}$$

$$\tfrac{1}{10} = .10$$

$$\tfrac{1}{11} = .09\tfrac{1}{11}$$

$$\tfrac{1}{12} = .08\tfrac{1}{3}$$

$$\tfrac{2}{3} = .66\tfrac{2}{3}$$

$$\tfrac{3}{4} = .75$$

$$\tfrac{5}{6} = .83\tfrac{1}{3}$$

$$\tfrac{3}{8} = .37\tfrac{1}{2}$$

$$\tfrac{7}{8} = .87\tfrac{1}{2}$$

$$\tfrac{11}{12} = .91\tfrac{2}{3}$$

A Selection of Lessons for the Sixth Grade

The Decimal System

The Decimal System is a system of reckoning by tens or tenths. Our number system is based on the number ten. Each number place to the left of the decimal point is 10 times the value of the place before it. Each place to the right is $\frac{1}{10}$ the value of the preceding place.

Common Fractions	as	Decimal Fractions
$\frac{1}{10}$	=	.1
$\frac{1}{100}$	=	.01
$\frac{1}{1000}$	=	.001
$\frac{1}{10000}$	=	.0001
$\frac{1}{100000}$	=	.00001

We know that

$$1 = \frac{10}{10} = 1.0$$
$$\frac{1}{2} = \frac{5}{10} = .5$$
$$\frac{1}{5} = \frac{2}{10} = .2$$
$$\frac{1}{4} = \frac{25}{100} = .25$$
$$\frac{3}{4} = \frac{75}{100} = .75$$

How would you find the decimal equivalent of other common fractions? Do you remember the rule?

Divide the Numerator by the Denominator!

Follow this rule and show that:

$$\frac{1}{3} = .33\frac{1}{3}$$
$$\frac{1}{6} = .16\frac{2}{3}$$
$$\frac{1}{7} = .14\frac{2}{7}$$
$$\frac{1}{8} = .125$$
$$\frac{1}{9} = .11\frac{1}{9}$$
$$\frac{1}{11} = .09\frac{1}{11}$$
$$\frac{1}{12} = .08\frac{1}{3}$$
$$\frac{1}{16} = .06\frac{1}{4}$$

It is convenient to know the following decimal equivalents as well:

$$\frac{2}{3} = 2 \times 33\frac{1}{3} = .66\frac{2}{3}$$
$$\frac{5}{6} = 5 \times .16\frac{2}{3} = .83\frac{1}{3}$$
$$\frac{5}{8} = 5 \times .125 = .62\frac{1}{2} \; or \; .625$$
$$\frac{7}{8} = 7 \times .125 = .87\frac{1}{2} \; or \; .875$$
$$\frac{11}{12} = 100 - .08\frac{1}{3} = .91\frac{2}{3}$$
$$\frac{15}{16} = 100 - .08\frac{1}{4} = .93\frac{3}{4}$$

Change the following common fractions into decimal fractions to the second place, showing the remainder as a common fraction if necessary:

$$\frac{5}{9} \qquad \frac{7}{9} \qquad \frac{4}{11} \qquad \frac{7}{11}$$

Spelling

Look up the meaning of these words, write it down and learn to spell them:

> decimal
> decapod
> decagon
> decalog
> decade
> decennial
> decimate

Percent Means Per Hundred

Last year we learned that it is easier to use decimal fractions than common fractions and that we can change common fractions to decimal fractions by dividing the numerator by the denominator,

Changing a common fraction to hundredths is to find its value per hundred, or the percent. Centum is the Latin word meaning hundred.

If one of you should get 12 out of 20 right answers in a test, the score as a common fraction is $\frac{12}{20}$. To find the percent score we divide 20 into 12:

$$\begin{array}{r} .60 \\ 20\,\overline{)\,12.00} \\ \underline{12.00} \end{array}$$

and find that $\frac{12}{20}$ = 60/100 (or .60) which is 60%.

Because $1.00 = 100¢, we most easily find a fraction of the dollar through hundredths, or percent (%).

$\frac{1}{100}$ of $1.00 is the same 1% of $1.00

1% of $1.00 = $.01 = 1¢

$\frac{6}{100}$ of $1.00 is the same as 6% of $1.00

6% of $1.00 = $.06 = 6¢

$\frac{10}{100}$ of $1.00 is 10% of $1.00 or 10¢

To find a percent of more than $1.00, such as 6% of $2.00, we can think: Since percent means per hundred, 6% means $\frac{6}{100}$ or .06.

6/100 of $2.00 is the same as .06 x $2.00

$$\begin{array}{r} \$2.00 \\ \times\ .06 \\ \hline \$.1200 \end{array}\ \text{ or } 12¢$$

Whether we want to find a percent of dollars, or of bushels, or of pounds, or of children, we change the percent to hundredths as a decimal fraction and multiply by it.

What are the steps in finding 20% of 30?

$$20\% = 20/100 = .20$$
$$.2 \text{ of } 30 = .2 \times 30$$

$$
\begin{array}{r}
30 \\
\times \quad .2 \\
\hline
6.0
\end{array}
$$

$$20\% \text{ of } 30 = 6$$

Taking these same steps find

25% of 16,   35% of 84,   90% of 250, etc.

(Let the children supply examples also.)

What Is a Mill?

You can usually find dimes, nickels and pennies in your purse but never a *mill*. You keep mills in your minds. If you are rich enough to own a penny, there you have 10 mills. A mill is $\frac{1}{10}$ of a cent.

As a decimal you write it $.001 to read it as $\frac{1}{10000}$ of a dollar.

You know that $.01 = 1\%$, so $.001 = \frac{1}{10}\%$

If 1 mill = $\frac{1}{10}$ of a cent = $.001 = \frac{1}{10}\%$
        2 mills = $\frac{2}{10}$ of a cent = $.002 = \frac{2}{10}\%$
        3 mills = $\frac{3}{10}$ of a cent = $.003 = \frac{3}{10}\%$
        $3\frac{3}{10}$ mills = $.0033 = \frac{33}{100}\%$
        $4\frac{1}{2}$ mills = $.0045 = \frac{45}{100}\%$
        $\frac{1}{2}$ mills = $.0005 = \frac{5}{100}\%$
        $6\frac{3}{8}$ mills = $.006375 = ?\%$

If 1 mill = $\$\frac{1}{1000}$
        19 mills = $\$\frac{19}{1000}$ or $.019, and that would be $1\frac{9}{10}\%$ of $1.00
        22 mills = $\$\frac{22}{1000}$ or $.022 or $2\frac{2}{10}\%$ of a dollar

What % of a dollar are 12 mills, 9 mills, 9.2 mills?

Fractional Percents

When you think in terms of mills, you can understand fractional percents, or fractions of cents.

$$\tfrac{1}{2}\% = .005$$
$$\tfrac{1}{3}\% = .0033\tfrac{1}{3}$$
$$\tfrac{1}{4}\% = .0025$$
$$\tfrac{1}{5}\% = .0020 \qquad \text{etc.}$$

$$1\tfrac{1}{2}\% = .01$$
$$3\tfrac{1}{2}\% = .035$$
$$2\tfrac{1}{2}\% = .022 \qquad \text{etc.}$$

Can you change the following from % to decimals?

If 10.3% = .103, how about 22.2%, 1.5%, 4.25%, 5.5% and such?

Introduction to Interest

What if Michael asked me to lend him 30¢ for carfare? What would you think of me if I were to say, "I'll lend you 30¢ but you'll have to pay me 3¢ a day for each day that passes before you pay back what you borrowed. If you take 7 days to pay it back, then you will owe me not only the 30¢ but 7 × 3¢, or 21¢, more—altogether 51¢. In other words I would charge Michael 10% of the amount of the loan, per day, a price for the *use* of the money. You would think I was taking advantage of Michael by making him pay back more than he borrowed.

You can imagine the plebeians of Rome coming home from a war. Their fields or shops have been neglected and need to be restored. They want to buy new materials but they have no money. They have not been paid to fight for Rome. They have to borrow the money they need and somehow manage to pay back more than they borrowed, just for the use of someone's money. If they can't, they are taken as slaves or put into prison.

This charge for the use of money loaned was called "usury" in earlier times, (Latin: *usuria*). People who loaned money and charged for the use of it were called "usurers" and they were much despised.

They had an *interest* in other people's troubles, not an interest to help the troubled ones but an interest in themselves and to make something for themselves out of others' needs. So the term usury came to be called interest meaning the amount the usurer charged for loans.

So if I charged Michael 10% per day for a 30¢ loan, that charge would represent *my* interest in lending him the money and by no means his interest in borrowing it, his need to ride instead of walk all the way home.

Interest, as a charge for the use of money, was figured as a percentage of the amount loaned which is called the *principal* amount. In ancient times the rate of the interest charged was high and was the reason why the poor, who had to borrow and who could not pay back the principal plus the interest, were punished by prison or slavery.

In Greece, Solon forbade selling men into slavery because they could not pay interest on their loans. In much later times the Jewish people and the Christian Church forbade usury among their own groups, that is to say charging high rates of interest. In later times low interest rates were permitted by law and it came to pass that people could both borrow and save money with interest.

What does this mean?

If a poor person, like you or me, needs money, it can be borrowed from a bank and paid back little by little at a rate of interest that is fair and lawful.

Or if a poor person wants to save money, he can loan it to the bank and the bank will pay him interest for the use of his money.

In Roman times it was usually the poor who had to borrow from those who had money. Today the banks are places where anyone can deposit money in a savings account and be paid by the bank for the use of such money.

Suppose you would put $100 in a savings account in a bank. The bank would pay you a certain rate of interest (maybe $5\frac{1}{4}$%) per year as long as you leave your money in the bank. How much interest would you earn in a year?

$$5\frac{1}{4}\% = .0525$$

Can you multiply $100.00 by .0525 and get $5.25?

Then your savings account would show a balance of $105.25 (the principal plus the interest), that is, of course, if you left $100.00 in the account for the year and unless you put more into your account during the year to earn more interest.

More Matters of Interest

Rent is paid for the use of a house.

Fare is paid for the use of a bus or a plane.

Interest is paid for the use of money.

Money is used to earn money through interest. When a bank lends you money, it earns the interest you pay. When a bank borrows your money, it pays you interest.

The money borrowed is called the *principal* (P, for short).

Interest (I) is the money paid for use of principal.

The "rate" of interest you pay is a percent of the principal over a certain period of "time."

If you borrow $100, and pay $5 interest, you have paid interest at a rate of 5%.

$$
\begin{array}{lll}
\text{Principal (P)} & = \$100 & \\
\text{Rate (R)} = 5\% & \times \ \underline{\ .05} & \\
\text{Interest (I)} & \ \ \$5.00 &
\end{array}
$$

The amount paid back = P + I = $105.00 and the rate is figured for a period of one (1) year, which is the *time* (T).

If Mr. Jones borrowed $600 from a bank at a rate of 6% per year, and paid the loan back plus the interest, how much would he have paid for the loan?

$$
\begin{array}{lll}
\text{P} & = & \$600 \\
\text{R} & = & \underline{\times \ .06} \qquad (6\%) \\
\text{I} & = & \$36.00
\end{array}
$$

We found the Interest by multiplying the Principal by the Rate. We can write the rule, which is called the FORMULA, as:

$$
\text{I} \quad = \quad \text{P} \times \text{R}
$$

Suppose that we already knew the Interest ($36) and the Principal ($600) and wanted to find out the Rate. How would we do it? $36 is a fraction of $600, isn't it?

$$\frac{\overset{6}{\cancel{36}}}{\underset{100}{\cancel{600}}} = \frac{6}{100} = .06 \text{ or } 6\%$$

What would the formula be for finding the Rate?

$$\frac{I}{P} = R$$

If 6% of the money Mr. Jones borrowed is $36, how much did he borrow? In other words, how could you find the Principal if you knew the Rate and the Interest?

If P × .06 = 36, then P and .06 are the factors in 36. You can divide 36 by the factor you know, .06, to find the other factor, P, which you don't know, the unknown number.

$$\frac{\overset{6}{\cancel{36}}}{\underset{.01}{\cancel{.06}}} = .01 \overline{)6.00} \overset{600.}{} = 600$$

Can you work out the formula for finding the Principal?

$$\frac{I}{R} = P$$

This Year? Next Year? Some Time?

Loans are not necessarily paid back in one year although the rate of interest is based on a year.

A builder borrowed $2500.00 from a bank to finish a house. He paid it back at the end of 2 years at 6% interest per year. How much interest did he pay?

$$
\begin{array}{rl}
P & = \$2500 \\
\text{Rate} & \times\ .06 \\
\hline
I & = \$\ 150 \quad \text{for 1 year} \\
T = & \times\ \ \ 2 \quad \text{for 2 years} \\
\hline
& \$\ 300 \quad \text{total amount of I}
\end{array}
$$

Taking Time (T) as meaning the length of time he took to repay the loan, we can see that

$$
I\ =\ P\ \times\ R\ \times\ T
$$

Mr. Smith invested \$1800 (P) and it earned \$225 (I) in $2\frac{1}{2}$ years (T). What was the rate (R)?

By using the formula we can find the unknown rate.

$$
\begin{array}{rcccccc}
I & = & P & \times & R & \times & T \\
\$225 & = & \$1800 & \times & R & \times & 2\frac{1}{2}
\end{array}
$$

In this problem you can divide the amount of the 2 known factors to find the unknown R.

$$
\frac{\overset{\overset{1}{\cancel{5}}}{\cancel{45}}}{\underset{\underset{8}{\cancel{40}}}{\underset{3\cancel{6}0}{\$1\cancel{8}\cancel{0}0 \times 2.5}}} \ =\ \frac{1}{8 \times 2.5}\ =\ \frac{1}{20}\ =\ 5\%
$$

What would the formula be?

$$
\frac{I}{P \times T}\ =\ R
$$

Problem: Find the Rate if P = \$700, I = \$52.50, T = 1 yr. 3 mos.

Mr. Smith's brother borrowed \$600 at 5% and paid \$75 interest. How long did he take to pay back the loan with the interest? Time is the unknown factor. Our formula would be:

$$\frac{I}{R \times P} = T$$

Can you work this out? Would it be $2\frac{1}{2}$ years?

If the Interest is unknown, we can find it by *multiplying* the Principal by the Rate by the Time.

$$I = P \times R \times T$$

If any one of the other factors is unknown, we can find it by dividing the Interest by the two known factors.

$$\frac{I}{R \times P} = T$$

$$\frac{I}{P \times T} = R$$

$$\frac{I}{R \times T} = P$$

Now you are ready to understand algebra in the seventh grade!

Simple Interest and Compound Interest

You may not think that what you have studied, so far, about Interest is very simple but it is termed Simple Interest.

An Example of Simple Interest

$$P \times R \times T = I \qquad P + I = \$104.00$$
$$\$100 \times .04 \times 1 \text{ (yr)} = \$4.00$$

Suppose that the Savings Bank adds an interest payment to your account at a rate of 4% per year every quarter of a year, that is every three months, and that you leave the interest in the account for the whole year. The Bank would pay you for letting it use both Principal and Interest. Your money would then be earning Compound Interest.

Compound Interest

January 1–April 1	$100	
	× .04	
	$4.00	*I*
	× .25	*T*
	20 00	
	80 00	
	$1.00 00	*I*
	$100	
April 1–July 1	$101	*New P*
	.04	
	$4.04	*I*
	× .25	*T*
	20 20	
	80 8	
	$1.01 00	*I*
	+ $101.00	
July 1–October 1	$102.01	*New P*
	× .04	
	$408 04	*I*
	× .25	*T*
	2040 20	
	8160 8	
	$1.0201	*I*
	+ $102.01	
October 1–January 1	$103.03	*New P*
	× .04	
	$4.12 12	*I*
	× .25	*T*
	20 60 60	
	82 42 4	
	$1.03 03 00	*I*
	$103.03	
	$104.06	*New P*

Commission

We buy most of what we need in small amounts from stores. The storekeeper, who is called a "retailer," buys what he needs to stock his store in much larger amounts from the people who produce or store the goods. These people are the "wholesalers" because they deal with even larger quantities of goods.

This is one way that it works. The dairy farmer milks his cows twice a day, early morning and late afternoon. The milk is poured into a large, sterile milk tank. It is collected by a milk dealer who comes with his tank truck and attaches a sterile pipeline to the farmer's milk tank and draws the milk into the truck tank. Then he takes it to his plant where he heats the milk to a certain temperature, not boiling, and cools it very rapidly and seals it in cartons as "pasteurized" milk. Some of the milk is homogenized, shaken so that the cream mixes permanently with the milk. That, too, is done by the dealer. Then the cartons of milk are distributed to various stores where we buy them. All along the way the milk has to be paid for.

The farmer (producer) gets a certain price from the dealer. Then, for the pasteurizing, homogenizing, packaging, and so on, the dealer has to get a higher price from the grocer. The grocer charges us more than he has paid to the dealer, to cover his expenses, such as refrigeration, until he sells the milk to us.

So it is that between the producer (farmer), the wholesaler (dealer) and the grocer (retailer), the price you (as the consumer) have to pay for the milk you drink has been raised twice since it left the farmer, once by the dealer and again by the grocer.

There are other situations where retailing plays its part. We can speak of agents or agencies that engage in selling something for someone else. There are artists' agents, literary agents, and automobile agencies. There are employment agencies where you can go for help in finding a job. They sell your help to an employer and you have to pay the agency a commission out of what you earn. There are rental agencies and the landlord has to pay an agency a commission for finding him a tenant. A person who sells something for someone else, be it art work or milk, is usually paid a percent of the sale and the amount he receives is called his commission.

Very often a wholesaler will hire a man called a "broker" to arrange sales of goods to retail stores. The wholesaler pays the broker, as commission, part of what he himself would otherwise get if he sold his goods directly to the retailer. For instance, the dairy farmer could get more for his milk if he did all the work of pasteurizing, packaging and distributing, but he has enough to do just taking care of his cows, his barn, the milking, the planting and harvesting of hay and corn, and many another chore. So the broker, in between the producer, the dealer and the retailer, is called a middleman. He has to earn a living too and in most businesses what he earns depends on how much he sells. He is paid on a commission basis. If he sells a lot, he earns a lot. If business is poor, or if he is a poor salesman, then he has a hard time.

Some Problems

Mr. Brown employs a real estate agent to sell his house for him for $25,000.00. The agent's commission is 5%. If the agent sells the house, how much will he earn as his commission? How much will Mr. Brown get as *net proceeds*?

$25,000	$25,000
× .05	− 1,250
$1,250 (commission)	$23,750 (net proceeds)

An orange grower sent 1000 crates of oranges to a broker. The broker sold them at $3.75 a crate. How much did the sale amount to?

$3.75
×   1000
$3,750.00   **$3,750.00**

The broker returned only $3,300.00 to the grower. How much did the broker earn?

$3,750
− 3,300   (net proceeds)
$ 450   (commission)

What was his rate of commission? $450 is what % of $3,750?

To find out, reduce the fraction   450/3750 to its lowest terms and divide the numerator by the denominator? Do you get .12 or 12%?

More Formulas

There are three! They help you to find the unknown figure in questions that have to do with sales, commissions and rate.

Finding Commission

If a sale (S) is $500, and the rate (R) is 5%, what is the commission (C)?

$$S \times R = C \qquad \$500 \times .05 = ? \qquad \begin{array}{r} \$500 \\ \times\ .05 \\ \hline \$25.00 \end{array} \qquad C = \$25.00$$

Finding Rate

If a sale is $2,750 and the commission is $660, what is the rate?

$$\frac{C}{S} = R \qquad \frac{\$660}{\$2750} \qquad \frac{66}{275} \qquad \begin{array}{r} .24 \\ 275\overline{)66.00} \\ \underline{55\ 0} \\ 11\ 00 \\ \underline{11\ 00} \end{array} \qquad R = 24\%$$

Finding the Sale

A fruit broker who gets 12% commission estimates that he must earn $300 a day to operate his business. What must the daily sales amount to?

$$R = \frac{C}{S} \qquad \frac{\$300}{.12} \qquad \begin{array}{r} \$\ 25\ 00.000 \\ .12\overline{)\$300.00} \\ \underline{24} \\ 60 \\ \underline{60} \end{array} \qquad S = \$2,500.00$$

Special Sales

The month of January is usually the time of the year when merchants want to get rid of stock that is left over after Christmas to make room for new stock coming in. For some reason they are called White Sales, perhaps because there is still a lot of snow falling. It's a good time for prices to fall, too. Merchants reduce their prices. The mark-down in price is called the discount and its rate is a certain percent of the pre-Christmas price. There are other reasons for sales, also. Can you think of any? Thrifty people wait for sales, look for sales, buy at sales, so as to save money. They are bargain hunters. They like to figure out what they save in terms of the rate and amount of discount.

Can you figure out some of these questions?

(Let P = regular price, S = sale price, D = discount, R = rate.)

At a store's 90th Anniversary Sale, the regular price of 1 gal. of paint was reduced from $6.98 to $4.89. What was the amount of the discount and what was the rate?

$$P = \$6.98$$
$$S = 4.89$$
$$D = ?$$
$$R = ?$$

Formula

$$\frac{D}{P} = R$$

A tire that usually sells for $31.00 is reduced by 9%. What is the sale price? Use the formula:

$$P \times R = D$$
$$P - D = S$$

A Book Club reduced the price of a novel to $2.97. The amount of the discount was $1.98. What was the price before the discount?

$$S + D = P$$

What was the rate of discount? Do you know the formula?

We have been learning about discounts at sales. There are other reasons for discounts such as buying in bulk, as from a wholesaler, let's say 500 lbs. of sugar instead 5 lbs; institutional discounts such as 10% off because you are buying for a school or a camp; cash discounts such as for paying cash with an order rather than paying when you receive a bill.

Tomorrow I will tell you about times when you have to pay *more* than the price of an item rather than less.

Taxes

Note: The facts and figures used in this discussion are from the 1964 World Almanac. You would have to up-date them.

In New York City everything that I buy costs me more than the price a store puts on its goods. (Almost everything!) Why? Is someone cheating me? No. You and I are paying for the services that our government gives us by paying taxes. These taxes provide the money which helps to run our city, state and national governments. There are sales taxes, a certain percent of the cost of an item is added to its price and these taxes go to your city or state government. There are with-holding taxes, actual taxes on your income, at a certain percent, that go to your state government (state income tax) and national government (federal income tax). In some states, such as New Hampshire, there are no sales taxes but there are property taxes based on the value of a person's property holdings. These taxes pay for services in the towns or cities, as well as public schools.

Governments have to be supported by their citizens. For instance, the government of New York City has to pay all the people who work for the city: the police, the park men, the street cleaners, the office workers, the Mayor, the Commissioners, the Judges, the School Teachers, the Janitors, the firemen. The city has to pay for fire engines, trucks, office equipment, lawn seed, and other supplies and equipment too varied to think of all at once. Just so, the state government has its expenses: salaries for the Governor, for the representatives and senators, the state police, the highway department, and so on. State salaries, per year, add up.

Governor	$50,000
Lt. Governor	20,000
Secretary of State	28,875
Treasurer	35,000
Attorney General	35,000

208 senators and representatives each paid $10,000.

The national government, upon which we depend for the most far-reaching help, has to have money to pay the President and all his assistants, the lawmakers in the congress, the federal judges, the FBI, the Army, Navy, Airforce and all their weaponry.

The taxes are established by law and by the elected representatives of the people.

A 5% tax on a restaurant meal is, in New York City, a city tax. A 15% tax on a ticket to a horse race is a city tax. A 3% tax on the price you pay for a car is a city tax. New York City taxes have to be authorized by the State of New York.

Some state taxes are: 10% on all jewelry you buy, 5% on airplane tickets, 5% on household appliances, 10% on opera glasses, field glasses or binoculars, 6¢ a gallon on gasoline. An automobile license plate costs anywhere from $15 to $20 per year and is a state tax. The amount depends on the weight of the car.

New York State taxes you on your income, for example:

2% on $1,000
3% on $1,001 to $3,000
4% on $3,001 to $5,000
5% on $5,001 to $7,000
6% on $7,001 to $9,000 and
10% on over $15,000

Some federal taxes are: 10% on tickets to movies, operas and theaters, on furs, luggage, telephone calls, pistols. Last year the federal income tax was 19% of your income. This year it was reduced to 14% at the request of the President and voted by Congress. Congress has the final power to impose taxes. The House of Representatives suggests the tax rates. They have to be voted by both the Representatives and the Senators and passed or vetoed by the President. If he vetoes a tax, it can still be voted by ⅔ of the Congress.

Some Quotes on Taxes

Joseph made it a law over the land of Egypt unto this day, that Pharaoh should have the fifth part.

—Genesis XLVII, 26

There went out a decree from Caesar Augustus that all the world should be taxed.

—Luke II, 1

Taxes are the sinews of the state.

—Cicero

Taxation and representation are inseparably united. God hath joined them; no British Parliament can put them asunder.

—Lord Camden, 1765

Taxation without representation is injustice and oppression. It brought on the American Revolution and gave birth to a free and mighty nation.

—Burke

Idleness and pride tax with a heavier hand than kings and parliaments.

—B. Franklin

The repose of nations cannot be secure without arms, armies cannot be maintained without pay, nor can the pay be produced except by taxes.

—Tacitus

A tax is a payment exacted by authority from part of the community for the benefit of the whole.

—Samuel Johnson

The thing generally raised on city land is taxes.

—C. D. Warner

His horse went dead, and his mule went lame,
And he lost six cows in a poker game;
Then a hurricane came on a Summer day
And blew the house where he lived away;
An earthquake came when that was gone,
And swallowed the land the house stood on.

And then the tax collector came around,
And charged him up with the hole in the ground.

—Author unknown

Ratio Equivalents

Every summer I have some hummingbirds feeding outside my window. I mix their food for them and put it in glass feeders. It is a mixture of honey and water. The recipe is 1 cup of honey mixed with 3 cups of water. How many cups of honey-water are there in the whole mixture?

The relationship between the amount of honey to the amount of water is what?

1 part honey to 3 parts water or 1 to 3 (1:3). I make such a mixture at least once a week for 12 weeks. How many cups of honey and how many cups of water do I use?

12 cups honey and 36 cups water.

There is the same relationship between the honey and the water whether in 1 week or 12 weeks.

1:3 is the same relationship as 12:36.

This relationship has a special name, "ratio" from the Latin word, *ratio*, meaning relationship.

The Ratio of Honey to Water, Week by Week
(draw and fill in)

Honey	1	2	3	4	5	6	7	8	9	10	11	12
Water	3	6	9	12	15	18	21	24	27	30	33	36

These ratios equal each other, are *equivalents*, just as you can have equivalent fractions. $\frac{1}{3} = \frac{2}{6} = \frac{3}{9}$, etc. But there is a difference of meaning.

$\frac{1}{3} = \frac{1}{3}$ of a whole. If I had 2 cups of honey water and $\frac{1}{2}$ was honey, $\frac{1}{2}$ water, would the ratio be 1:3? No. The ratio would be 1:1, honey to water. If the ratio is 1:3, honey to water, the amount of honey is $\frac{1}{4}$ the amount of the whole and the amount of water is $\frac{3}{4}$ the amount of the whole and there is $\frac{1}{3}$ as much honey as there is water.

If you get $\frac{4}{5}$ of the words correct in a spelling test, does that tell you how many words were in the test? Could it be 20 words, 100 words? Does it tell you how many words were right, how many were wrong?

More Equivalent Ratios
(draw and fill in)

Number of words right	4				
Number of words in test	5	10	20	50	100

Change the following fractions to their simplest form:

$$\frac{8}{10} = \frac{4}{5}$$

$$\frac{16}{20} = \frac{4}{5}$$

$$\frac{40}{50} = \frac{4}{5}$$

$$\frac{80}{100} = \frac{4}{5}$$

$\frac{80}{100}$, or 80:100 has the same ratio as 4:5, whatever the whole.

$\frac{80}{100}$ as a fraction actually means 80 out of the whole amount of 100, or 80%. However, if we think of the percent as a rate, and change the spelling from R A T $\underline{E}$ to R A T $\underline{I}$ $\underline{O}$, then we can understand the meaning of a ratio between numbers.

A ratio is a comparison of 2 numbers.

Compare 2 numbers, such as 6 and 4 or 6:4:

$$6 \text{ is } 1\tfrac{1}{2} \times 4$$

Compare 12 and 8:

$$12 \text{ is } 1\tfrac{1}{2} \times 8$$

Compare 9 and 6:

$$9 \text{ is } 1\tfrac{1}{2} \times 6$$

We can say: 6 is to 4 as 12 is to 8 as 9 is to 6. They are equivalents.

Made in the USA
Columbia, SC
07 March 2022